A genuine brother a loyal friend we will always keep your name alive your style & grace was so superior how you touch lives & the friends around you but now you sitting up high like a real King where you can't be touched I will always remember your comical side a true blessing to the world.

Shavar Jamal Lewis

(Doody)

December 28, 1977- March 22, 2015 R.I.P

THIRTEEN GOING ON THIRTYFIVE

THE J WILKINSON STORY

THE SPECIAL EDITION

WRITTEN BY: GOD-SON

TABLE OF CONTENTS

CHAPTER ONE- THE MOVE

Brought into this world as Rakim Jones I was raised a country boy. Born on October 18, 1978, the third oldest of six children. My stepfather was there along with mama so in all it was eight of us. In a small house that matched the tiny town of McComb, Mississippi, we had become a tight knit family. We stuck together and everybody loved one another and worked hard.

By the time I was four I had become used to the country life. At night I listen to the crickets in the field from the bedroom I shared with my brother and sister. During the days we played in the pastures all day. When I found out that my step dad and mama had plans to move, somehow I knew things would never be the same.

In the summer of 82' our family packed up and moved all the way to Rochester, New York. Miles away from the country fields, the farms and all the animals everything felt different. The houses were so close together I could see inside the neighbor's house. This was certainly a big change. At four years old I was in a whole other world. I had come from country fields to big buildings and bright lights. We had to move in with family while working to save money to get our own place. All these transit buses and fast moving traffic everywhere is new to me and my family. I was in awe for the next few months.

While out walking one day me and my older brother, Marvin walked by the local Boys & Girls club where we see kids breakdancing on a card board box. They were spinning on their heads and backs, dressed in Adidas sneakers and Adidas sweat suits, looking real fresh. They all danced to the music pumping from a big radio that rattled the sidewalk. Their moves were captivating. I was so amazed that I instantly fell in love with it. I had never seen nothing like this in my life. Again, I was awe. As Marvin and I slipped off from the breakdancing crew all I could remember was the beat of the music and the kids spinning on their backs.

Finally we make it home and as I walked through the door, I couldn't wait to tell mama what I had seen on my first real venture through the streets of New York. My mama was so happy I had seen something that I admired. Within a couple months of us staying with family, my mama and step dad found us an apartment on the West side of town.

My step dad was a very hard working man but he was also very strict. Mama always made sure me and my five siblings had what we needed in life and not what we wanted. She had six kids, three boys and three girls. We all are pretty much different. Me, I love the sound of music. It's just something about it that motivates me. Since hearing the sound of that beat coming from the radio, I have been stuck on this hip hop thing.

A few months later after watching nothing except the four basic channels that was on television, we finally get cable. My brothers and sisters and I were happy that day. While watching television intently one day, I learn there is a show called 'YO MTV Raps' that plays hip hop videos. That Saturday morning while watching the show, a video comes on by a rap duo called Eric. B & Rakim & the song is called 'How Can I Move the Crowd.' It sounded like magic to my ears and from that moment I had fell in love with hip hop and the state of New York.

Fast forward a couple years and I am now eight years old, and hip hop has become a big part of my life. I now have my own collection of cassettes, or at least Marvin did. My brother didn't mind if I borrowed his tapes as long as they were returned. Reciting rhymes from Biz Markie, Fat Boys, Big Daddy Kane, Heavy D, just to name a few.

The kids at my school were into hip hop as well and through the music I made a couple of friends. One memorable day while walking home from school with my sister Michelle, my older brother Marvin and a couple of our friends I watched the happenings as I listened to my head phones, bobbing to my music. As we get closer to our house and approaching the corner of Genesee Street, we see these guys huddled up on the corner. What looked to be a hoodlum dressed in all black runs up on the crowd with a hood covering his head and pulls out a big black 357.

He screams out. "Alright motherfuckers yawl know what time it is, run it everybody!"

I watched in confusion as the stick up kid smacks one of the drug dealers across the face with the gun and immediately blood starts pouring from his face. Quickly the other victims hand over their jewelry and money, except one kid. He tries to snatch the gun from the man and in the middle of the tussle the gun goes off and the stickup kid shoots him in the face twice. Blood flies everywhere and the kid drops to the ground leaking like a faucet. Everybody runs and scatters leaving the kid face down murdered in cold blood. The scene was horrific. It was the first murder I'd ever witnessed in my life, yet it wouldn't be my last. As we walk pass the murder scene my big brother looks down at me with a worried expression.

My sister looks at us and says. "Welcome to the big city of dreams everything in New York ain't always what it seem."

The next day I walk down and finally joined the Boys & Girls Club. I figured the more time I spend inside of there, the less time I'd spend out of the street and probably out of trouble, too. Once I became a member I was hooked on going there because they played the hip hop music that I loved at the center; hip hop was everywhere. On my way walking home from the Boys and Girls Club one day I see this strange writing on the wall of the store on the corner of Lennox St. with big letters and designs. I later find out that its graffiti. It's a part of the hip-hop culture that's growing and I am very interested in it.

One day I'm sitting in my room looking out at the park and there it is again, the kids with the sweat suits break dancing with the music blasting from a big boom box sitting on the park bench. I lift up my window and all I can hear is...

"Hip-hop started out in the park we use to do it out in the dark." They are playing a song by MC.SHAN.

By this time I am getting very familiar with the hip-hop scene. I even started to write rhymes here and there. I'm growing and learning more about this hip-hop culture.

As me and my older brother venture out into our new neighborhood, I notice there are hustlers on every street corner with new clothes and jewelry looking fly like the rappers that I see on TV. I want to be a part of that so badly, but I'm still just a shorty right now.

Each time I walk pass the corners, it was like watching a movie. The crack heads looked like zombies as they walked the streets. Every now and then I'd see the neighborhood girls hanging around the hustlers who flashed their cars and jewelry. They looking like superstars riding in Benz's and Range Rover trucks. To me this was the life! The hustlers in my hood always stayed shining like a diamond.

Sitting in class one day, I notice this kid drawing the words Kid-1, which looks like the spray painting that I saw in my old neighborhood called graffiti, except the kid is drawing it on paper with a pencil.

"Yo, how you do that?" I asked the kid intrigued by his art.

He replies with a strong New York accent. "Wdup son, my name Shamar."

"I'm Rakim , I'm from Mississippi."

"Oh this," he said. "It's easy to do. You just sketch the big letters into whatever you are trying to spell."

So I try it later that day during our class free time, and just like that I had done my first graffiti tag. After school Shamar and I walk home from school, and as we get to talking we realize that we live on the same block. As we approached his house I gave him a fist pound.

"Thanks for teaching me how to draw that graffiti. I'll see you tomorrow."

Shamar grinned. "Cool, son. I'll get with you later."

As soon as I walked into the house, my mama has a surprise for me. I looked past her smiling face and see a brand new set of turntables, a microphone and a couple records. As I look through all the records I see The Fat Boys, Biz Markie, M.C. Lyte, BDP, KRS 1, and LL Cool J. I hug my mama so tight she can hardly breathe.

After dinner, Marvin helps me hook up my new D.J. equipment. I put the first record on, its KRS1. I hear the sound roaring from the speakers 'SOUTH BRONX, SOUTH BRONX' I'm so excited I scream through the microphone.

"Wdup this is D.J. Rakim live in the flesh."

The vibe was so real it feels like I'm a part of hip hop now. I spent my whole night spinning records until I fell asleep. The next morning I am awakened by Shamar screaming up to my window.

"Yo, Rakim!"

I lift the window. "Yo, I'll be down in a sec."

After getting dressed, Shamar and I take off walking up the block. There it is again like a flash back. The hustlers up on the corners looking fresher than a new Benz, rolling dice playing the game 4,5,6. I was truly intrigued by all their jewelry and their nice cars parked alongside the curb.

"Yo Shamar, wdup with those cats always posted on the corner?"

"Those are what ya call hustlers, drug dealers. They getting that money, son. They deal weed, coke, and heroin. Whatever ya looking for they will sell it to ya."

This was nothing new to Shamar, because his entire family used and sold drugs. It was in front and around him every day. I still didn't know what being a hustler meant. All I know is they dressed fly as a motherfucker. I was picking up on a lot of new slang. The things that I wouldn't normally see back in my hometown, I am picking up on while living in the big city.

The sun is going down and it's starting to get late. I can feel the sprinkles from the rain starting to fall and then I hear a loud thunder.

I look at Shamar. "Yo, it's time to head home before the weather gets bad."

As we walk down the block in the mist of the rain trying to hurry home I can see the lightning in the sky.

I give Shamar a pound. "I'll holla at you later."

"Later, son," Shamar replied before running to his house to get out the rain.

I try to make it home while the weather isn't too bad. As I'm walking down the street listening to my headphones, I see these two guys run up on a clean black 745 BMW with chrome wheels and windows tinted. The two guys open fire on the driver side window. When the bullets spit out the barrel, I could see sparks of fire coming from the tip of the gun. The windows shatter as they continuously fire shots at the car lacing the driver with bullets.

I was stuck and I couldn't move. I see the driver gasping for air trying to breathe as he is choking on his own blood. One of the shooters opened up the driver side door, pulls the driver out the car and pistol whips him with the gun. He puts three more bullets in his chest after snatching his jewelry off his neck and committing the crime, he takes off running with his partner. I dropped my head and kept walking acting like I saw nothing. I was scared as shit! I couldn't hide my fear for much longer so I began running home in the pouring rain.

Puzzled about what I just saw I didn't know if the man died, but from the looks of it all I would assume he did. I was lucky I didn't get shot! I walked in the house taking deep breaths. My sister Michelle must've saw the fearful expression on my face.

"What's wrong Rakim?" She asked as she stood in front of me.

"I...I just saw someone get shot up on the corner," I replied as I wiped the rain off my face.

She looks down at the floor solemnly. "That's the second one in a couple days."

"I know wow this is crazy," I replied shaking my head.

My sister walks off to tell my momma what happened and I head up stairs and jump in the shower. As I get out the shower it's thundering even louder. I can feel the house shaking. I turn on my music and try to master how to make these blend tapes. They are called blend tapes because in order to do this correctly, I have to blend the other record in before the first one goes off. It's like mixing the two records together. After blending and mixing for a few hours, Marvin walks in and shows me a set of hair clippers.

"Rakim, I've been learning how to cut hair, and I have a tablet with a lot of graffiti and drawings in it. I am going to learn how to carve these design's in people's heads with my new set of clippers," he informed me with excitement in his voice.

"Yo that's hot big bro, you'll have people lined up for haircuts in no time."

He smiled earnestly. "I have been practicing Rakim."

While talking to Marvin I started falling asleep, but the crackling sounds of lightning and thunder keeps scaring the shit out of me. The lights are going on and off. I can hear my little sister and brother down stairs screaming, scared of the thunder boom that keeps knocking the lights out. All of a sudden there is a lot of banging at the door. Marvin and I run down stairs and see momma opening the door. My Aunt Matty falls in hitting the floor dripping wet. She's screaming at the top of her lungs saying my uncle just tried to kill her by throwing her in the Genesee River. My mom takes her in the back room and tries to clean her up.

Just as we all tried to settle down there is another loud knock at the door. I accidently opened the door before I checked to see who it was. That was a big mistake. Now I was standing face to face with my Uncle Sam. He doesn't know that my aunt is in the back and he starts screaming that he killed my aunt.

Matty walks out the back room and when they see each other Sam points and angrily snarls. "Bitch I thought you was dead!"

He charges Matty and tries to grab her. My step dad runs from the back room, grabs him and takes him outside, while my mom keeps my aunt calm. After getting the situation somewhat under control Mama sends all us back to our rooms.

I gasped as my heart pounded. "Marvin did you just see what happened? That was crazy, looked like something out of a movie!"

The next day rolls around and I see my aunt and uncle back together again. My mama looks at my step dad and says "I guess that's love."

He shakes his head and replies, "Two damn fools is what that is."

CHAPTER TWO- TEMPTATIONS

I wake up early and get dressed the next morning. I head down stairs for breakfast with my backpack, ear phones and a couple mix tapes that I'd made.

I greeted Mama in the kitchen as I grabbed my breakfast. "Good morning, Mama?"

"Good morning Rakim," she replied as she stirred something on the stovetop. "Leaving already?"

"Yeah," I said as I ate my food standing.

She caught me before I could get out of the kitchen. "Rakim how are thing's going for you?"

"Life is good Mama. I can't complain. I will talk with you later I'm headed over by Shamar's."

She looks at me and says, "I guess you're in a hurry young man."

I didn't reply making my way to the door like I was running late for work or something. I put on my headphones, listening to this new RUN-DMC tape as I made my way up the block. Trying not to think about what I saw yesterday, I don't even look in the direction the scene took place. When I glance up, I see Shamar hanging out near the corner.

He yells out, "Yo wdup son?!"

"Yo, ya not gonna believe what I saw yesterday," I exclaimed while approaching.

"What?" Shamar asked eager to hear the news.

"I was half way down the block and saw this kid get shot up and murdered, just after you went home last night."

"Yeah, I heard about it, that's just something you are going to have to get familiar with here in New York. These streets are grimy," he informed me.

"Yea I'm starting to see that."

"Yo, what you listening to in them earphones, Rakim?"

"It's the new EPMD."

"They are okay," Shamar says.

I laugh and say, "ya know ya like EPMD."

"Na I'm, an Erick B. & Rakim fan!"

"Yea they're dope too," I agreed.

I take my shirt off. "It's hot out here," I said as I used my hand to wipe the sweat from my brow.

"Yea son, it's going to be a long, hot summer."

Shamar's older sister Bridget walks out the house, "Shamar you ready to get your hair braided?"

"Yea I'm ready, yo I'm a catch up with you later, Rakim."

Since Shamar had gone inside to get his hair braided, I decided to go to this record store Marvin had told me about. I walked up to the corner of Webster Avenue and waited. Finally after fifteen minutes a city bus pulled up. I paid a dollar to ride, found a seat on the back and continued to listen to the mix tape. After another fifteen minutes I had reached my destination. I step off the city bus and walk inside Midtown Plaza. I see people everywhere inside the place. I catch the escalator up to the second floor and walk into the record store.

There are so many records everywhere to choose from. I walk over to the hip hop section and start scanning through every album they had. I see an album by a familiar group that I saw on T.V. called A Tribe Called Quest. They are one of the hottest groups out so I grab that record, and an album by Slick Rick. After browsing a few more records, I decided it was time to head home.

I jump back on the city bus and a matter of moments it drops me off at the corner of Garson Ave. As I jump off the bus my street is like a live block party. The Spanish people are out cooking and selling shish kebabs and chicken on the corner. The drug dealers are all over the corners, while the loud music is playing in the back ground. As I head down the block I see Shamar hanging out and talking to a pretty girl with his hair freshly braided to the back.

He spots me and screams out, "Yo, wdup Rakim!"

"Wdup Shamar."

"What you bout to do?"

"I'm heading to the house to make a couple mix tapes."

"Aight fam." Shamar says before giving me a fist pound. "Check you out tomorrow."

I get home and crank up my music, my big brother walks in the room looking fly like the hustlers on the corner.

"Yo wdup D.J. Rakim" shouts Marvin,

I notice his eyes are glossy red like he's high.

"Nothing I'm just cooling, playing around with the music. Yo, where you get them new fly clothes and sneakers from?" I ask Marvin.

He just smiles and says "I can't tell you now but things are about to get better, just be cool."

He leaves right back out after grabbing something from the closet. I don't look too hard, so I act like I'm in to my music. Marvin is in and out the house a lot and my mama notices it but keeps quiet. As Marvin leaves one day I go through his closet and find two big zip lock bags full of weed and a bunch of little bags with white powder in them and a loaded chrome 38 caliber gun. There is a knock at the door I close the closet door quick and run down stairs.

It's Shamar. "Yo wdup son!"

"Just chilling playing around with the music, come on up."

We go up to the attic and I instantly show Shamar what I found in my brother's closet.

"Yo, you hustling already?"

"Na son, this not my shit this is Marvin's, I found it in his closet."

"Yo your brother's a hustler like them cats on the corner. Let me get some of that weed," Shamar eyes grow as he looks at the big package.

"What are you going to do with it?"

"I'm going to roll it up and smoke it. What you think?"

"Yo Rakim let's go get a Philly blunt from the corner store up on the Ave."

I agree and we leave the room with just enough weed to get high off of. I didn't want Marvin to know that I had been snooping in his stuff. As me and Shamar approach the corner store, I was shocked to see my big brother Marvin posted up on the corner. He was looking fly as a motherfucker, dipped in jewels like Rick the Ruler.

"Rakim well I guess we know where the new clothes and stuff in the closet came from."

I look at Shamar, "yo I never would've thought."

We walk back to Shamar's house and sit on the back porch. While he's rolling up the blunt I'm still in a daze about my brother and the whole hustling situation. Shamar lights up the blunt.

I say to him, "Yo, Shamar you smoke like you done this before."

Shamar just blows the smoke out through his nose and smiles, "here you go son, hit this shit and relax."

I hit the blunt and start choking. My mouth gets watery and hot.

"Hit it lightly, not hard Rakim."

After a few puffs I get the hang of it and I'm starting to like the feeling the weed is giving me.

"How you feeling over there Rakim?"

"I'm good, I'm high as a kite, feeling real mellow."

As the sun sets, you can see the city lit up with lights. The streets still busy like it's day time. Every now and then you hear a couple gun shots and police sirens, but that's just a part of the New York life. Early the next morning I meet up with Shamar on the corner to sell a couple tapes.

"Yo, Rakim, you got some more of that weed from yesterday?"

"Yea I got a little"

"Let's go snatch a Philly blunt out the store."

As I hustle my mix tapes to the drug dealers for ten dollars apiece, Shamar sits back and rolls the weed and admires my street hustle. I put my earphones back on and count my money up.

I snatch the earphones off amazed. "I just made a hundred dollars in five minutes."

"Rakim, what if that was coke or weed it would have been five hundred in five minutes."

I looked up at him and smiled while wiping the weed ashes from my clothes "Yo, that ain't my style kid, the streets ain't ready for a drug lord like me."

"I hear you Rakim. Let's go hang out at Peck Street Park."

While sitting in the park listening to music in my headphones I spot the prettiest girl in the city, looking fly with a pretty smile. Still high from the blunt we just smoked, I walk over to her.

"Yo, wdup sexy, my name Rakim but you can call me Rah. I see you checking me checking you."

She smiles and says, "I'm Boo, I just moved here from the south."

We exchange numbers after a few moments. I'm really feeling Boo's style.

As she walks off she turns around and says, "Don't forget to use that number."

"Trust me I won't!"

Shamar shouts, "Yo, look at that Benz on them twenty inch chrome rims."

I just gaze at the Benz with the plush cream leather seats. Yo Rakim, that's the biggest drug dealer in the hood his name is Power. He moves more bricks than any hustler around the hood. He has a crew of killers that roll with him."

I watch as Power parks and gets out the machine. His linen is flawless with more jewelry on than Mr. T, looking flyer than a 747.

He walks over. "Yo, wdup shorty, I hear you got them mix tapes for sale."

"Yea I got five left."

"Let me get all of them, hey wdup Shamar" says Power.

"I'm good, I like that Benz I see you out here splashing on these niggas, huh Power?"

"You two little niggas can splash too, all you got to do is fuck with me."

"Na we don't rock like that. Thanks for the offer, though. We bout to head back to the hood."

Power shouts. "One love yawl, be safe."

As we walk back down the block I say, "yo Shamar these streets are tempting but I don't want to get caught up out here."

"Yea Rakim I hear ya, but it's the life we live every day. Where we live is a constant fight to stay alive nah mean but for the record I do rock like that you might not."

"I hear ya."

"Well, I'm in for the night Sham get up with you later."

As I step inside, mama greets me in the kitchen. "Well, how was your day Rakim and how's the music coming?"

"I can't complain, everything is falling in place. I've been doing real good selling my tapes."

"That's good son, keep up the good work Rakim be careful out walking these streets. I just saw on the six o'clock news a young kid was shot and murdered over on Hudson Ave today."

"I will keep that in mind, mom. Well I'm headed up to take a shower and play with the music, talk to you later."

As I head up Marvin walks in the house with his jewelry and new clothes looking all flashy. Mama stops his ass at the bottom of the stair case.

"Son, me and you need to sit down and have a little talk."

"What's up mom?" Marvin asked.

"You tell me son do you think I'm crazy? I notice that you're coming in and out the house all times of the night. You are coming in here wearing these fancy clothes and jewelry and I damn sure didn't buy them. Now, where the hell are you getting the damn money from?"

At this point I walk past them, but I can still hear their words. Marvin drops his head in shame and in a low voice mumbles "I've been hustling."

"Hustling what Marvin?"

"Weed and coke."

Mama begins yelling at the top of her lungs, I can hear her way up stairs in the attic. I run back down to make sure everything is alright.

"Son, I didn't raise no drug dealers. I don't want that shit in my house, what kind of examples are you setting for your younger brothers and sisters. You are going to wound up dead or in jail. I don't have no bail money to come get you out and I damn sure don't have no money to bury you. I'm gonna tell you this one time son. You better leave them damn drugs alone and get your education."

"Yes ma'am" replies Marvin.

As he walks upstairs in shame I follow him up.

"What's wrong big bro? You look like somebody just put a gun to your head," I asked as if I wasn't listening to the argument.

"Mama found out I been hustling dope out on the block and she wasn't very happy about it."

"I knew you was out there hustling getting them paper stacks."

Marvin looks at me with an evil eye. "I know one thing I bet not catch or hear about you out there hustling trying' to make no paper stacks. Make sure you go to school and leave the hustling to me."

"Yea, yea I hear ya. So what you gonna do now ?"

"I can't stop the hustle now Rakim, my paper is just starting to stack." He looks at me. "You can't tell mama about me hustling out on the block. Keep this between the two of us and I will make sure you stay looking fly for the little girls at school."

After his words, we both just fall out laughing.

The next day while hanging out at the park selling my tapes, I spot a cherry red Lexus sitting on a pair of sparkling shiny rims with the windows tinted out dark. The car pulls up on the side of me the windows roll down.

It's X and Power. "Yo, wdup kid?" Shouts Power.

"Yo, wdup Power? Yawl know me I'm just out here hustling these tapes."

The two jump out. X is looking real fly and fresh. He has on a big chain and a scorpion pendant hanging around it, he looks at me smiling knowing that I want a piece of the action. Then he passes me the blunt.

"You need to hop in this ride and get this money with us."

As I sit back and pull on the blunt I remind him. "Yo, I told you that ain't my style."

Power says, "I hear you Rakim, we gone get back on the grind. We'll holla at you later baby boy."

As I watch them pull off I think about the jewelry, the clothes and the cars. Even though I know it's wrong the temptations are driving me crazy, but I know I need to stay focus out here in these streets. I have to do the right thing. While walking up the side walk I see Marvin cutting one of his friend's hair out on the front porch. I look at it real close, he has cut the guy's name in the back of his head (Howie.D) and has it looking sharp and neat.

"I'm next," I shouted as I approach them.

After his friend gets through with getting his hair cut I sit down. "Yo Marv give me a Caesar with the New York City buildings carved in the back."

He gets through and it looks illmatic. I'm really feeling this haircut.

"Yo,big bro I think you gone be the best at this kid you got me looking fresh over here."

Before we knew it he has customers lined up everywhere trying' to get a fresh haircut. The people are coming so fast the clippers don't have a chance to cool down. My brother was making money from every angle and I respected that about him.

CHAPTER THREE- INTRO TO THE STUDIO

While chilling out at the park one day, listening to my headphones, a guy walks up to me and asks, "what you listening to shorty?"

"I'm listening to Naughty by Nature, a new rap group," I replied still bopping my head.

"Do you know how to rap?"

"I do a little bit."

"My name is Magic Mike," he announced as he gave me a handshake. "I make music, take my name and number, and call me some time. Maybe you can come by the studio."

I took the number and stuffed it deep in my pocket; I was so excited thinking I am actually going to a real studio. While listening to my headphones and sitting on the park bench, watching the drug dealers roll dice from a distance, I hear an advertisement about a concert. Snoop Dogg, Dr. Dre, The Dogg Pound, Warren G, and Lady of Rage were coming. The announcer said, whoever wrote an essay on how they would make the world a better place; they could win backstage tickets to meet and greet all the rappers before the show.

I said to myself, "that can't be too hard to do; I need to get started soon as possible."

On my way back to my hood, I see the police flying through the city with their lights and sirens on. I wonder what could be going on. As I reach the corner of my block, the police have all the local drug dealers lying on the ground searching their pockets, looking for drugs. I was so glad I didn't see my brother, Marvin laid out being searched; mama would've killed him if he would have been on that corner. All the bad things that happen in my neighborhood remind me to stay focused and out of trouble. I walk straight upstairs to my room in the attic. As soon as I get home I prepare to write this essay. The whole time I was writing, the only thing that I kept thinking about is me having a chance to meet these superstars. By now it's ten o'clock at night and I've been working on the essay for four hours straight. I think I've got it about wrapped up.

Early the next morning I call up to the radio station and get the address so I can put the essay in the mail, and then I head to the corner to drop it off in the mail box. Now that I got that out the way it was time to call Magic Mike and see about getting in the studio. It's nice outside everybody's on their bikes, and all the kids are getting wet with the water from the fire hydrant. I see a friend of mine from school. He has on these new fresh black Jordan's with a polo shirt and polo shorts to match with his gold chain on that has his name 'Byrone' on it. He and all his family are from Jamaica.

Byrone asks me, "why you not out here hustling? I see ya boy Shamar out here stacking that paper, you need to get down."

"Yeah it sounds all good," I replied. "But I'm a let yawl have that, I'm hustling these mix tapes, why don't you cop one from me?"

He just laughs and pulls out a stack of money and buys one. I'm saying to *myself "damn that money looks good."* I give him a pound and head out.

"Yo I'm a catch up with you later rude boy."

I stop at the corner pay phone to call Magic Mike, and the phone rings like five times before he answers.

"Yo wdup, this Magic Mike."

"Yo this is Rakim, the kid you met at the park. I'm trying to come by the studio."

"Can you stop by next Saturday, about ten a.m.?"

"Cool no problem."

We hang up and I post up on the corner watching the hustlers roll dice. I decide to walk over to the crowd and everybody has big stacks of money out in their hand yelling *"BET THE FIVE."* It's money all over the ground. It looks like about five grand is down there. Out of nowhere Shamar walks up.

"Yo son, what are you doing up here with the hustlers rolling dice?"

"I'm just cooling. Just got off the pay phone, try'na win this contest on the radio to meet Snoop Dogg, his whole crew coming here to do a concert. Yo, where you been? Haven't seen you in a couple days?"

He just starts smiling. "Yo Rakim, I heard on the radio about that contest too, I hope you win son. I've been out here chasing this paper though."

"Yeah I hear you Sham, you be careful out here. The police came around earlier today laying the whole block down, searching them for drugs and guns."

"Yeah," Shamar says, "it's hot out here. Everybody is trying to hustle and the police circling every five minutes."

"Yo Rakim, you think your mom will let me stay at your house tonight?"

"Nah she won't mind, it's cool."

I look over at Shamar, "yo light that blunt up kid I see you holding it."

As we sit up on the Ave smoking, we see the police and ambulance flying to the other end of the block.

"Yo son, lets walk and see what's going on down there."

While I'm hitting the blunt, I see the crowd getting bigger. I look and it's my friend Little Jay. He's laid out on the stretcher with my home boy Shawny.B standing by his side he accidentally shot his self in the dick. That's when I realize guns were not for playing with.

We walk into my house, head up stairs to order some food and put on some music. A very loud thunder shakes the house. I look out the window and it's lightning. Then the rain starts to pour down very hard. As I'm looking out the window I see the pizza delivery guy at the house across the street. Soon as he gets out the car, a kid walks up with a black hoody on his head. He puts a gun to the delivery guy's chest and digs in his pockets taking all of his delivery money.

Seeing these types of things in my neighborhood was starting to be normal. It also makes me more conscious and aware of the choices I need to make in life. Just as the rain pours harder, Marvin walks in drenching wet, he pulls out four stacks of money.

"Wdup Rakim, wdup Shamar?"

While taking off his wet clothes. He pulls a gun out his coat pocket and puts it in the closet.

"So what's been up Rakim?"

"Nothing much, I'm headed to the studio in the morning to see about this little rapping thing."

"I hear you little bro, well I'm about to take a shower and get some sleep. Catch up with you two tomorrow."

I get up early Saturday, it's hustle day. I got my book bag with my tapes and my headphones as I step off the porch. Everyone's out early and, as soon as I get to the corner Shamar is already out hustling.

"Yo I'm headed to the studio son, catch up with you later."

Moments later I arrive at the studio. Mike is waiting patiently for me. There is all this music equipment, mixing board and lights. I'm blown away from hearing the sound of hip hop for the first time being in the studio, where it is actually created. Mike shows me all the equipment and lets me hear a lot of different beats and sounds.

"Yo Rakim, go in the booth and play around on the mic for a while. After about an hour Mike comes in and lets me hear a couple beats and tells me to pick out a couple that I like. He puts them on a cassette tape.

"I want you to write to these beats and come back to the studio next week for a studio session.

I was like, "cool" but I was so excited at the same time.

While chilling in the park later that day I see my big brother and a couple of his homeboys playing Cee Lo dice and guess who's smack dab in the middle? Sham. He's the smallest one out the bunch playing with the big boys. The Jamaicans are even out in the park today blasting the reggae sounds of Marley. In the park you can smell the weed drifting through the air.

Power pulls up at the park in a white pathfinder truck and jumps out all jeweled up with two of his goons on his side in case any drama comes his way. He gives everybody a pound, and then puts a hundred on the dice game; he's got so much money in his hands it looks like he's holding a green brick. Shamar walks over to me and hands me the blunt.

"Yo what's popping son, how did the studio session go?"

"It was cool; I go back in the studio next Saturday to do some recording."

Shamar looks up at me and starts smiling. "So you wanna be a rapper?" He then pulls out a stack of money and says, "This is what you need to be rapping about Mr. DJ Rakim."

I just looked at him in a jokingly way and said, "Just say no to drugs."

We both start laughing. "Yo, Sham, I'll catch up with you later. I'm about to walk up to the corner store."

I get up on my block and walk in the store and order me a Philly cheese steak sub with boss sauce. You can hear the Arabic music playing all throughout the store. As I walk out the store, my homeboys Doody and Jay Dog are letting their two pit bulls fight each other out on the corner with a 200 hundred dollar bet up in the air. I look across the street and see my Mama walking home from work. She works at a sewing factory in our neighborhood.

"Wdup mom?"

"Nothing, just ready to sit down get off my feet and relax."

As we walk in the house, the phone is ringing off the hook. I run and catch the phone. They are asking to speak to Rakim Jones. The man shares the good news with me once I announce my name.

"This is the radio station, 104wdkx and we are calling you to let you know that you have won the essay contest on 'How you would change the world.' You will receive a back stage pass to meet all of the members of The Dre and Snoop Dogg, Chronic Tour."

I was so surprised my face lit up like the fourth of July and I forgot to tell the man thanks. As I hung up the phone, I ran to the kitchen to tell my mother that I had won the tickets to the rap concert.

She just smiles and says, "that must have been a good essay

Rakim."

I head up to the attic to listen to the instrumental beats that Mike had given me to write to. I hear Marvin down stairs talking to my step dad.

As soon as he walks up to the room I swarm him with my good news. "Yo, I won the contest to go to the concert to meet all the rappers back stage. So I need you to give me some cash for an outfit and some fly kicks."

"Rakim, don't worry about that. Take this three hundred in cash."

I watch as he pulls four big zip lock bags full of weed out of a book bag and stashes it in the closet.

"Yo Rakim, don't forget what I said. You don't hear nothing or see nothing."

"Yeah I hear you Marvin."

* * * *

It's early Sunday morning, mama is cooking breakfast, I can smell it all through the house, and the aroma has woken everybody up. My little brother and sister had beaten everybody to the kitchen. These were the good times for the Jones family, just a good Sunday morning breakfast with everybody under one roof. As I get dressed I put on my New York Yankees hat and headphones. I steal me a little of Marvin's weed and walk down stairs. I see the news is on TV. A drug dealer was tied up in his basement and shot execution style then set on fire on the west side of town last night. As I walk out the door I just say to myself I wonder what I will be faced with today.

As I walk up the street busting down my Philly to roll me a blunt, I see Power coming. He's driving a new blue Honda Accord today. He slows down in front of me. "Wdup Rakim, come take a ride with me."

I jump in the car and light up the blunt. "Yo Rakim, I see you a smart kid. You stay fucking with your music and never let all these other kids out here influence you to fuck with these drugs."

"Yeah Power, too many young kids getting shot and murdered out here over these drugs. I'm still a shorty! I'm trying to live my life!"

"Yeah I respect that." He pulls the car in a drive way and says "yo Rakim get out with me for a second."

We walk into this house not too far from the neighborhood; Power leaves me in the kitchen then comes back with a big brick of coke and puts it on the table.

"That's a half a key, have you ever seen one of those?"

"Nah, this my first time."

He gets a scale and starts weighing up little chunks of coke and wrapping them up in plastic bags. When we get ready to leave he puts a forty five gun in his waist.

"Yo Rakim, can't let these stick up kids out here catch me slipping."

We get back in the car and Power drops me off in the park .Before he pulls off he yells out. "Yo, Rakim, whenever you get ready to make this paper let me know kid."

As he pulls off I take a seat on the park bench roll up more weed and put on my head phones. I start writing to the beats I got from Mike. After sitting in the park for two hours, Shamar pulls up in a green Range Rover. I walk over to the truck.

Shamar calls out. "Yo, get in Rakim!"

"Where you get this truck Shamar?"

He just starts smiling and says, "It's mine."

I look and see the key ignition is broke and back up from the truck. "Yo Shamar, I'm not fucking with you and that stolen truck."

"It's not stolen. I got to go, I'm on the move. I'll catch up with you later Rakim."

I put my book bag on because it's starting to get late. When I walk in the house I can hear Blues music playing in the background my aunts and uncles talking noise to each other. They come over a lot on the weekends to drink and play cards; we have a packed house every weekend, which was another one of the Jones family good times.

CHAPTER four-THE CONCERT

Two more days until the concert and I'm about to jump on the next city bus that comes up the Ave. I needed to hit Midtown for a pair of fresh sneakers. As I get on the bus I see Ms.Shirley is driving today. She doesn't charge me for riding the city bus. She's a nice older lady that lives across the street from me.

"How are you today, Rakim?"

"I'm doing good, how are you today Ms.Shirley?"

"I'm fine."

As I jump off the bus, I see it's packed downtown. Everybody is getting ready for the concert. I go into a store called 'All Day Sunday' to pick up a hooded sweater, and get my name stamped across the front of it. As I'm walking through Midtown Plaza I look up and I see the rappers Kurupt and Daz of the group, Dogg Pound walking in the mall. I was overwhelmed at the sight of them. I can't wait to see them perform at the concert in two days. I walk into NYC Fashion's next, to get a Guess outfit and a pair of Travel Fox shoes. I bump into my Jamaican friend Byrone; he's all jeweled up looking fresh.

"Wdup Rakim? How you son?"

"Everything good, I'm just picking up an outfit for the concert."

"Yea it's gonna be hot."

"Tell me about it. Yo Rakim, I got my peoples waiting so I'm a get with you later."

"Alright peace son."

I can't believe all the people that are out today shopping, getting ready for the concert. I see a lot of the hustlers from my neighborhood out getting fresh for the concert. While waiting for my bus, I see two of my brother's friends B. Blast and Boe-Cat. They pull over and give me a ride back to the hood. They pull over and let me out on the corner of Goodman St. I walk across the street to Garson Ave and there is a fight going on, one of the hustlers named, Markus just knocked out a crackhead in broad day light, for not paying him. I see Shamar coming up the side walk.

"Yo wdup Rakim?" "Cooling, just coming from downtown. Yo Sham you got a Philly? Let's roll up this blunt and go sit on your front porch. Yo son you need to stay out them stolen cars. That shit not cool."

"Hey, I know man. I was just having a little fun, yo."

"Yeah, well don't let having a little fun get you locked up."

Bridget walks out on the porch, that's Shamar's big sister. She says, "Wdup Rakim? Let me hit that blunt."

"Nothing just cooling bout to get ready to go to the studio."

"Alright rapper," Shamar joked with me.

I hit the blunt before I walk off. "Yo Shamar I will catch up with you later. I'm about to head to the studio for a couple hours."

When I get to the studio there are a couple of guys getting ready to leave. Mike is amped up. "What's been going on Rakim? You got your rhymes memorized? You ready to record?"

I nodded and go inside the booth with the microphone. Mike turns on the beat and I put on the head phones. Mike gives me the go ahead and I just start rapping over the beat. We work on one song for three long hours. I didn't know you had to put this much work into rapping. Finally Mike gets all the sounds the way he wants them and plays the song back so I can hear it. As I'm sitting I can't believe that's my voice rapping over the beat. I'm proud of myself. Before I leave, Mike gives me a copy of the song. "Yo Rakim, meet me here next week, same time for another session."

"Okay, peace Big Mike."

I put the tape in my Walkman and listened to it through my head phones over and over, walking back to the hood. I see Marvin hanging out on the block around the corner on East Main Street. He's got this big chain on, rocking a blue, jean outfit. He's hanging out in front of one of his drug spots.

"Where you coming from Rakim?"

"I'm just leaving the studio, heading home."

He pulls out a big bank roll and gives me a couple dollars. "Rakim, go straight home and stay out of trouble."

The sun is starting to go down, and as I turn the corner onto my block everybody's still out running up and down the street. Shamar shouts as I approach.

"Wdup Rakim, you finally made it back!"

He's shaking some dice in his hand enticing me to play. I'm fairly familiar with how to roll the dice from watching the hustlers.

Shamar chuckled and then says, "Let me roll this blunt up and get this dice game going."

We start off shooting a dollar. Next thing I know we are gambling for five. I'm up almost hundred dollars. I'm talking a lot of smack to Shamar while I'm winning his money. By the time night fell I had won a hundred and fifty dollars.

"Yo Rakim, its beginners luck."

"Yeah whatever nigga. Yo I'm bout to go home and count your money up son."

Shamar shrugs and say, "I'm staying at your house tonight Rakim."

"Cool." I smiled while counting my money.

I'm up early the next day; it's the day of the concert. They're talking about it all over the radio. The whole city is excited!

I wake Shamar up. "Yo we gotta get on the grind early today."

I count my cash up as me and Shamar make our way up the sidewalk. We stop in front of his house and roll up a blunt. We sit on the porch for a few minutes and get high early before we start our grind. The hustlers are pulling out their nice rides on the block, for the crackheads to wash them up to look nice for today.

"Yo, I'm bout to walk up to the barber shop on Goodman and get a haircut." "Yea no doubt, I'm about to let Bridget braid my hair. Meet me back up on the Ave later."

As I'm sitting in the barbershop there is so much hype and talk about the concert tonight. All I can think about was when I first moved to New York from Mississippi. Being so excited seeing kids breakdancing in the park, and watching the culture as it grew. Finally I'm done getting my hair cut and walk out the barbershop. I see Power pull up front in a Q45 leathered out, pearl white paint job with rims. This nigga has money and knows how to floss with it.

He hops out and greets me. "W'dup Rakim?"

"I'm just chilling Power, about to walk back to the Ave and see what's popping."

"Okay be cool little man."

I walk in the corner store and get a quarter juice and two Philly's. I see the hustlers and they got a dice game going on. I'm still feeling lucky from my first game with Shamar, so I drop five dollars down. I roll the dice and I hit 4, 5, 6, and won. Thirty minutes has past and I count my money up. I done hit for three hundred dollars. I can't believe it; I came up off five dollars!

I see my man Shamar coming up the block. "Yo I just won three hundred from the dice game," I reveal flashing the knot of cash.

"Rakim you just got beginner's luck son."

"Yo, Shamar I'm about to head home and chill for a little while. I will meet you at your house about six to catch the bus to the concert."

"Cool," he replied as he brushed a hand across his freshly braided hair.

I walked inside the house and I see my mom is sitting in the kitchen. She asks, "So, Rakim, are you ready for the concert tonight?"

"Yes I can't wait, I get to meet all of them back stage."

"You just make sure you be careful walking around downtown tonight," she warned with her warm eyes set on me.

I go upstairs to put on some music, and relax for a couple hours before getting ready for the show. When the clock strikes five o'clock I take a shower and start getting dressed. I put on Marvin's gold chain with the scorpion medallion and steal some of his weed.

As I made my way down the stairs I called out. "Mama I'm about to

leave."

"Be careful out there tonight, Rakim."

Shamar and I walk up to the bus stop and its people everywhere. We jump on the next bus; it's so crowded you can't even sit down. As we jump off the bus downtown I'm amazed! I swear I have never seen so many people in my life! All these fresh cars, everybody dressed up with their jewelry on. It's so much commotion with the loud music going on my head seems to be spinning.

"Yo Shamar I gotta go in through the back. That's where I have to meet the radio station people at."

"Okay, I'll get with you inside," he replies before disappearing in the big crowd of people.

As I walk through the back of the building, they give us these back stage passes that we all place around our necks. Next, they take us to a room and I can't believe it. I see the whole Snoop Dogg crew, all the rappers are sitting in the room. I see everybody from their whole crew; all these niggas look high as hell. They sit us down and commend us on our job for winning the essay contest. They answer our questions and tell us to enjoy the show and walked us out into the stadium. You could just hear the crowd roaring. I go to the concession stand to meet up with Shamar.

I yell out. "Yo wdup kid, let's go find our seats."

I see just about everybody from my old neighborhood from across town on the west side and all my friends from school. We find our seats, and the lights go out. It looks like about fifty thousand people are in here. Dre and Snoop come out on stage and the crowd goes crazy. They perform and rock the crowd for about forty five minutes, and then The Dogg Pound comes out and the lights are flickering on and off with smoke shooting all over the stage. Their appearance alone just makes the crowd go crazy. It seems like the stadium is shaking.

As the show is about to come to a close Snoop gets ready to leave off stage, they tell everybody to stop the violence and everybody be safe. We walk outside and it's packed. Police are everywhere and all of a sudden about three fights break out and we hear about seven gun shots. *So much for Snoop Dogg's warning,* I thought. The crowds are running and screaming. Sham and I run to catch the bus going towards our house.

We hop on out of breath from the long sprint. The whole ride we talk about the concert and the commotion that happened. Ten minutes later we get off the bus at the corner of our block. Its late night, but we still stop and sit on Shamar's porch to roll up a blunt. There are lots of people walking down the street coming from the concert. You can just hear everybody bickering and talking about the fighting and shootings that happened after the concert.

"Well, Shamar I'm about to head to the house, get up with you tomorrow"

"No doubt Rakim be safe".

As I walk in the house, I see on the news about the shooting after the concert. One kid gets shot in the leg fighting over who's from the East side and who's from the West side of the city. I just shook my head in disbelief as I watched the screen. I was beat so I dragged myself upstairs and went straight to bed.

Early the next morning I smell mom's breakfast wafting through the house. As I make my way in the kitchen to fix something to eat I see mama.

She asked, "How was the concert?"

"It was good, except for a few knuckleheads at the end of the show."

"I hope they didn't ruin it for the good fans," my mom said shaking her head.

A knock at the door got my attention. I look out the door and it's Shamar. I open the door and he steps inside.

"How you doing Mrs. Jones?" Shamar greeted my mama as he gives me fist pound.

"Fine and you?" she smiled.

"I'm good, what's up Rakim?"

After breakfast we head upstairs and as I'm getting dressed, Shamar pulls out a plastic bag with about thirty little baggies of coke.

He says, "It's time to start getting this money."

"Yo, kid, I told you that shit ain't for me."

"I know, son. I'm just making sure everything is there. This is my hustle now."

We bounce from the crib and while I'm sitting on the corner I just watch how everybody's getting money except me. My man Little Jay walks over and says, "wdup Rakim, you wanna hit this blunt?"

As I'm puffing, I'm seeing Shamar run back and forth to cars getting his money. It looks so easy like there was nothing to it. Everybody has on fresh crisp kicks, new clothes, jewels hanging around their neck with stacks of money in their pocket.

"Yo, Jay I'm a catch up with you later. I'm bout to head to Peck Street Park."

When I get to the park I'm sitting on the park bench and notice there is a couple people in the park today doing their own thing. I put on my headphones and start writing a couple rhymes in my note pad. My home boy Tim walks up "wdup Rakim?"

"I'm just cooling, wdup wit you, Tim?"

"Yo we got a shopping trip going to the city all up through Bronx, Queens, and Manhattan next month. You need to get your paper stacks right and stay in tune with me."

"I'll definitely do that. I need to make that trip."

"Alright, peace Rakim get with you later little bro."

I pull my blunt out and blazed it up put my headphones back on and kept writing. Just the sparkle from the hustler's jewelry, the crispy linen that they are wearing and the fancy ass cars parked in the park, knocks me off focus from writing so I get up and go to the studio for a couple hours.

"Yo Rakim, I'm really loving how you starting to craft the art of writing your music. You stay out them streets, you gone be the next big thing popping off in Rochester kid."

Thanks Mike, hey I'm a catch up with you next Saturday."

"Alright, peace Rakim, stay out of trouble."

CHAPTER 5

TASTE OF THE DRUG GAME

The bell rings, school is out and all the kids are racing to the front door. Only a couple more weeks of school left. Next year I will be in middle school. As I make it to my block I see one of my brother's friends named X. He's out here hustling today.

"Yo wdup Rakim?"

"Nothing I'm just coming from school."

"Yo Rakim, where Shamar been at?"

"He's locked up for stealing cars; he will be home in a couple more months."

"Yo, X, let me hit that blunt before I take off."

"Here you go shorty."

I take a couple puffs put my headphones on and get back on my mission. I walk in the house and flop on the couch. Rap City is on. They are playing this new video by Snoop Dogg. I head upstairs after the video goes off and look in Marvin's closet. Being nosey I see that he has three pounds of weed in a sack. I say to myself; if took enough to make me a little money and hustle with he'll never know. So that's exactly what I did. I run to the corner store and buy me some little plastic bags to bag the weed up. I start breaking the weed up but it's sticking to my hands, so I get some scissors and start cutting it up.

Finally I'm done chopping up the weed. I start bagging it up and I'm stuffing each little bag with weed. I get through and count the bags. I have forty five bags; two hundred and twenty five dollars in all. I put them in a sandwich bag and pushed them in my pocket. I walk back up to the corner; X is still up there.

"Yo wdup Rakim?"

"Yo X ,look what I got for sale, some nickel bags of weed."

"Let me get five of them for twenty," X asks as he holds out the twenty dollar bill.

So I give him five bags of weed and he gives me a twenty dollar bill. Before I knew it I was halfway out. The hustlers bought most of the weed from me because they sold mostly cocaine so there was really no weed around. I walk in the corner store to get me a sandwich and while I'm waiting for my food X walks in the store. A guy walks in behind him with a hood on his head wearing a strange look on his face. He swings on X and almost punches him in the face. X throws the potato chip rack in front of the guy, he trips, and falls and pulls out a gun. We run out the store and make it about a hundred feet before we start hearing gunshots coming from behind us. We see a car coming up the street driving fast; it tries to run us over. We run down a side street and start jumping fences. I jumped about eight fences, never stopping until I made it to my house. My heart was pounding like crazy. When I walk in the house my mom looks at me strangely.

"What is going on out there?" she asked.

"All the grownups are trying to get their kids in the house cause of the gun shots that just went off in the neighborhood," I replied meekly.

I wait about two hours till things cool down and I walk back up to the corner. I see X, he looks at me and just started laughing. "Yo, what was that all about earlier?" I asked.

X shakes his head. "Them cats was trying to rob me and you. They had been watching us the whole time we was out on the block hustling."

He lifts up his shirt showing me his chrome 38 in his waist band letting me know he was ready in case trouble popped off again. My first day trying to hustle and I almost got robbed and shot by somebody. These streets are wicked.

"Rakim you got to be strong out here on these streets, little niggas is getting murdered every day in the streets. Always expect the unexpected in the drug game."

As we are talking, Power pulls up flexing real hard in the black Benz. X is a part of Powers crew.

"Wdup Rakim, I see you hanging up on the block."

"Yeah, I got them nickel bags of weed for sale."

"I knew it wasn't going to be long little nigga, let me get six of them."

Now I'm out of weed I just made $225.00 in three hours. I got to figure out how I'm a get some more weed, I don't know who to talk to about getting it. Then it all hit me.

"Yo Power?" I called out before he could pull off with X.

"What's up shorty?"

"How much weed can I get with $225.00?"

"I don't fuck with that weed I fuck with coke. Let me talk to my Jamaican friend, give me the money I'll be back through in an hour."

True to his word Power pulls back up in an hour. He jumps out and hands me a paper bag.

"That's a quarter pound Rakim, if you need something else I will connect you with my boy dread."

I go home to break the weed down and bag it all up. I made $450.00 dollars off of the $225.00 that I spent for it. I stash the weed in the closet and turn on the radio. They are playing this new artist by the name of 2Pac; I'm glued to the radio. He is like a fresh breath of air for this new hip hop era. It's been a long day; I jump in bed while my little brother Pooh is falling asleep playing the video game.

About 2:30 am in the morning there is someone banging at the door. I run downstairs and my mom opens the door. It's one of Marvin's friends; he tells my mom that Marvin has been shot. She just goes into a panic mode looking for her keys, and she ties a red bandana around her head. Next thing I know she's burning rubber in the streets. She left my step dad and everybody else. I was at a loss for words, because I never thought in a million years that my big brother would get shot.

She finally comes home at about 8:00 am. She says Marvin's okay; but he is still in the hospital.

"Mom what happened?"

"Rakim someone tried to rob him. He didn't give them what they wanted, so they shot him. But the doctor's says he's going to be okay."

Later that day we get dressed to go to the hospital to go see Marvin. As we walk in the room he's asleep. He hears us walk in and wakes up. He just looks at everybody and says, "W'dup."

He looks like he is in a lot of pain. The doctors come inside and change his bandages. The police come in to ask Marvin a few question and if he knows who shot him. Marvin looks up.

"I don't know who shot me they had hoods on their heads."

The doctor walks back in and interrupts. "Marvin you can go home tomorrow. It looks like your wound is healing just fine."

We make it back home and I have a studio session with Mike at two o'clock. I get my book bag headphones and leave. When I pass up the Ave, I see my big homey Moosie.

He's out getting that paper today.

"Yo Rakim, I heard you got that weed. Let me get five bags from you."

"Cool I got you fam. Yo, Moosie, I'm a catch up with you later when I get back from the studio."

As I'm sitting in the studio, Mike wants me to record a song with this other kid that's from my neighborhood, his name is Jason. We record for four hours and knock two songs out. Mike replays the song's back and says he is impressed by our commitment to writing lyrics.

On my way home I stop by my friend Jerome house; him and his family are from Kingston, Jamaica. His mom comes to the door with a strong Jamaican accent.

"How are you doing today? Come in Rakim."

I can hear the loud rumbling reggae music coming from upstairs. When I get up stairs, Jerome's older brother Ervin is spinning some reggae tunes. "Yo w'dup Jerome, everything good?"

"Rakim, w'dup with you?"

"Not shit, looking for your brother Byrone.

Jerome replies "he's in the bathroom."

He walks out and I pull out a plastic bag full of weed.

"That's w'sup Rakim, give me three bags of the ganja, rude boy."

"Yo Byrone, I gotta get back to the hood. Tell your brother Horace I said w'dup."

"I'm a get with you son, be safe."

I cross Parsells Ave and finally make it back to the block. I see the whole crew up on the corner, everybody looking fresh and clean out hustling today.

"Yo Rakim how is Marvin doing? I heard he got shot."

"W'dup Bugs? Yeah, some stickup kids tried to rob him, he doing good fam. He's coming home tomorrow."

"No doubt that's good to hear."

"Rakim, when we find out who shot Marv we gone murder them kids; let 'em know we gone serve and protect out here."

"Yeah, no doubt I will let him know. I'm a catch up with you later Bugs I'm bout to step."

It's been a long day, but I finally make it home. I'm tired from recording music and smoking weed all day. I followed the smell of food to the kitchen.

"W'dup mom?"

"Nothing much Rakim, about to finish up cooking in a few minutes. I'll be picking Marvin up from the hospital tomorrow so clean that room up."

"Ok cool mom, I will take care of it."

I put on some reggae tunes as soon as I get in my room; it always relaxes my mind while I'm cleaning up. I finally get through cleaning and sit down and count my hustle money up. I got almost $500.00. I put my stash up, after dinner turn the light out and get in bed for the night.

The morning comes and I'm up at 6:30 am to get dressed for school. Today is the last day of school. I'm 13 years old and I will be leaving school #33 and going to Jefferson Middle School for the seventh grade next year. Just that fast I forgot that Marvin comes home today.

At the end of the day when school lets out kids are flying everywhere; it's going to be a long hot summer. It doesn't take me long to get to the house. As soon as I walk in from school I speak to my mom.

"Wdup mom, where's Marvin?"

"He's up in the room watching TV, Rakim."

I run up stairs. "Yo, w'dup Marvin?"

"Nothing much, Rakim."

"I'm just cooling, how your leg feeling?"

"It's good, just a little pain."

"Yo, everybody been asking about you up on the block, they told me tell you they on the lookout for that kid that shot you." He just grins.

I paged Power, and he calls me right back. "Yo I need a half pound of weed."

"Cool, meet me up at the store on Goodman Street in two hours."

Two hours later, I head to Goodman and we go upstairs in the building over the store. Power looks pressed for time, but he has the weed package for me.

"This is a half a pound Rakim; its 600 so you owe me 100. Better yet don't even worry about it. You good peoples we even fam."

"Alright thanks a lot, peace Power."

"One love Rakim."

I walk down to my house and bag the weed up in my room. I just look at the big ass brick of weed. Shit, after an hour I was already tired. It took me two hours to bag all the weed up, now it's time to flood the block and get this paper.

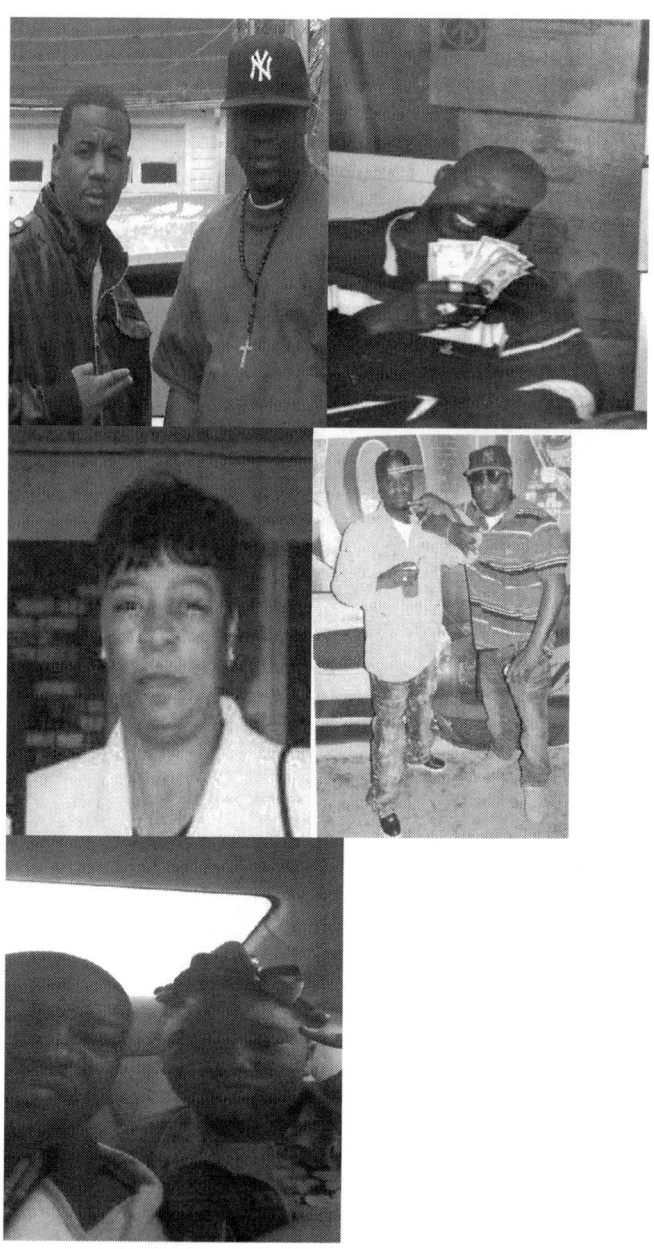

CHAPTER SIX A LONG
HOT SUMMER

As the summer started to set in, the hustler's began to flex hard in their clean rides. All the cute girls are out walking up and down the block. I have been on the corner hustling all day. I made about $700.00 today but the other hustlers out here selling have made like $1,500.00 dollars today. I walked down by Shamar's house to smoke a blunt with his sister Bridget.

"Wdup Rakim?"

"Not shit, bout to smoke this blunt with you. W'dup with Shamar, when does he come home?"

"He will be home in three more weeks."

"No doubt, I can't wait for that kid to come home."

"This some good weed, where you get this from Rakim?"

"I got it from some dread."

"Yo, let me get two nickel bags before you leave."

"No doubt I got you. Yo Bridget I'm bout to head to the house. Hit me up if you need some more weed."

I step in the house and walk up the stairs to my room and start going through Marvin's closet to see what else I can find. There's a plastic zip lock bag full of little white balls of coke. I go down stairs and get a plate a spoon and two round balls of coke out of the zip lock bag. On the street they are called eight balls. I set the two eight balls of coke on the plate and crush them with the spoon, until it all forms into powder then I cut a sipping straw with scissors on an angle and scoop the coke up and bag it all in little baggies. When I finish bagging the coke I make 260 off each one. All together I bagged $520.00, now it's time to hit the block and get some fast money.

As I get up on the corner I see it's booming. A crack head walks up to me and says "I need a fifty."

I give him five bags of coke. The traffic is so heavy up on the block that I'm going to be out of coke in a few hours. I see Power pull up across the street at the store, looking fresh rocking his jewelry.

"Yo w'dup Power?"

"W'dup lil Rah?"

"Nothing just cooling, yo I need to get some coke."

"Hold on little Rah, let me run in the store right quick."

Power steps out the store. "Yo, Rakim jump in the truck."

"How much money you got?"

"I got thirteen hundred."

He pulls up at this house and we go inside. When we get in he pulls his gun out his waist and puts a little brick of coke on the table.

"This is an ounce of coke, it weighs 28 grams. Give me twelve hundred and you should make about twenty two hundred off of this. You got to get you a beeper Rakim so you can keep up with your money. Take my number hit me up if you need something else."

"Cool, yo drop me off close to my house, down on Garson."

I jump out the truck a couple house's down from mine and take the coke upstairs and stash it. It's Friday night, my uncles, aunts and cousins are all over tonight playing cards. The blues music is up loud; everybody's drinking and having a good time. I walk back up to the corner store and get a pack of plastic baggies to bag the coke up in. Before I head back I stop and smoke a blunt with my big homey Ed.

"Yo Rakim, I seen you up here earlier today getting that money little nigga be careful out here shorty. I don't know what's going on out here, Rakim. Power and his crew act like they don't want me out here hustling on the block. I saw him in the barber shop and I tried to talk to him, but he act like he didn't even know me."

"Yo, Ed, everything cool just be easy big dog, it's enough paper out here for all of us to eat without getting rowdy."

"Yeah no doubt Little Rah, you a cool little dude. I like your style."

"Yeah, well I'm a check you later big homie, I'm bout to walk to the house and bag this blow up."

The next day I'm up on the block hustling and guess who I see, my little homey Shamar walking up the side walk. "Yo w'dup kid, you finally made it home!!!!."

"Yeah son! Yo Rakim, I see you out here all jeweled up, looking like you getting that money. Life must be good."

"I'm just trying' get what I can get. Let's roll up, and politic it's been a long time."

While Shamar and I are sitting on the corner, Markus walks up. He's a part of Powers crew. "W'dup Shamar when you came home kid?"

"Just made it this morning."

"Good to see you fam."

I look up and see Ed and another kid walking out the cut, both of them have strange looks on their face while they're eyeing Mark.

"Yo Markus, walk off before they try you."

"Nah fuck them."

I look up at Ed, he just has a blank look on his face. Mark flinches and then the kid with Ed pulls out and both of them start firing shots. Mark pulls his gun off his waist and starts firing back. I take off running; Shamar slips and falls as we make it to the next block. Me and Shamar start checking ourselves to see if we had been hit.

"Damn Rakim, sound like about twenty shots went off."

We go sit on Shamar's porch till the smoke clears and walk back up to the corner. Out of all them shots fired I can't believe nobody got shot.

"Yo Shamar look at all these bullet holes in the apartment building from the shootout."

"Hey Rakim, I haven't been home a whole day and this is what I come home to."

"Sham come walk down with me to Biz Mart on Webster Ave to get me a beeper."

"Damn Rakim, you getting money like that."

While in Biz Mart I see my man Lil.B (Byrone). "Wdup rude boy?"

"Cooling."

"Rakim I just got my new rims put on the Honda and painted it brown with the flakes in it"

"Yea I see you blinging out here."

"Yo Lil.B, tell O.G. Puk I said hope he get well soon. I heard he caught one in the stomach."

"I will. Yo Rakim yawl be safe."

"Yo Sham, I got an ounce of coke left at home, we can go bust it down tonight and bag it up. I will give you half of it and help you get back on your feet"

"Cool."

When we make it back to my house, the news comes on and I see one of my friends name Charles. I sat next to him in class. He had been hit and killed by a train while walking home one day with his family. I could not believe what I just saw. It stunned me to see my friend that I went to school with lose his life so young. We head up the stairs to take care of our business by getting the coke bagged up.

"Yo Shamar, lets walk up to the corner get a Philly roll up and smoke one for my boy Charles that just passed away."

"No doubt we definitely can do that."

While sitting on Shamar's porch, it's dark out. I spark the blunt and all of a sudden crackheads just start coming out of nowhere. The block is hot tonight!

"Yo Rakim, we gonna chill out here all night til we get this money. We got to get us a gun in case those stick up kids try to run up and put us in a jam baby boy."

"Yeah we need to work on that."

As the night passes the money is still coming.

"Shamar I got to get home before my mom starts thinking something is up. I'm a catch up with you tomorrow, hold it down my nigga."

As the sun rise the next morning I'm up like I have a job. My beeper is going off and that means money. I get fresh, throw on my baggy jeans a pair of Timbs and walk around the block to make a hundred dollar sale. Then head over by Sham's house.

"Yo, w'dup kid, we got to get some more coke I'm almost out."

"I got a hook up with this Jamaican kid name Dangles. He does business with my brother.

I got his beeper number so as soon as we get this money counted up we can call him up."

"Yo Rakim, check this out. I bought this chrome 38 revolver last night from my cousin."

"Yeah that's sweet. You hit somebody with that motherfucker, you gone make his ass Harlem shake. Yo go put that up. Let's try to get some coke so we can stack some paper today and go shopping."

I call up Jamaican Dangles to bring us an ounce of powdered coke. A few minutes later he pulls up on us real low key with a strong Jamaican accent.

"Yo Rakim, you owe me $1200, Mon."

"Here you go that's 12, everything there rude boy."

"Yo, Rakim hit me up if you need any ting else Mon."

We hustle hard all that day trying to catch every sale we could. The cops rolled by every hour checking the block out, making it hard to get this money. A couple weeks roll by and I have my money stacked up. I bought lot's of clothes and shoes; I can't front this has been a good long summer.

While sitting out on the block I see, Precious heading my way with Dinnique and their little walking crew.

"Hi Rakim!"

"Wdup Dinnique?"

"I see yawl out here looking pretty patrolling the side walk today."

"Shut up Shamar, you think you funny."

"Yo, Dinnique when you gone be Mrs. Rakim?"

"Ha ha real funny. Yawl need to get off the corner fake hustlers."

Check out that Lexus dripping with candy paint Sham, that's them boys off Parsells and Stout them cats getting that money, too. Yo Shamar you got the gun on you?"

"Yeah I got it."

"Is it loaded?"

"Yeah."

"Let me see it, let me unload it right here while it's dark outside."

I point the gun in the air and let off five shots. There so loud I believe it made two of the street lights go out. Five minutes later the police are flying up and down the block with their lights on.

The pull over. "Hey you kids, seen anybody out here shooting a gun?"

Shamar looks up. "No Officer."

We both watch as the police officer pulls off slowly. I look at Shamar and laugh. He shakes his head.

"Rakim I'm bout to go inside before you get us locked up. Catch you on the flip side."

CHAPTER SEVEN - MUSIC OR THE DRUGS

The school year will be here soon and the end of summer is approaching. "Hey mama, I'm headed to the studio for a session. I will be back later."

When I get to the studio Mike sits down and we start chatting.

"Rakim what's been going on? I have been hearing some bad things in the streets about you. Word is you're out there hustling. You are too young to be out here in these streets. You're gonna have to pick either the streets or the studio. Now get in that studio and spit that heat, and stay focused on the music and not the hustling."

After three hours of recording, I'm back in the hood doing what Mike told me not to do. Hustling somehow it has become addictive. As I step to the corner there is an unfamiliar face hustling up on the block.

"Yo, Rakim who is this kid?"

Shamar starts reaching in his jacket "I don't know you nigga, what you doing up on our corner?"

"Yawl two little fuckers better go sit the fuck down for I blast you little niggas."

"Yo Shamar go get the gun."

"I already got it."

He pulls out and points the gun at the kid. His whole conversation changed. "I'm bout to leave."

"Yeah that's what the fuck I thought, before you get your face shot off!"

"Yo, Rakim, that's what's gone happen to anybody that ain't from the block if I catch they ass up here hustling. I'm bout to go up on Hudson Ave and do a drop off. I'm a catch up with you later kid.

Soon as he walks off the block it goes to booming again. The money is coming so fast I can't put it in my pockets fast enough.

"Yo wdup big bro? Haven't seen you in a couple days."

"You know me Rakim, I'm a paper chaser but what are you doing up here on the corner looking like you hustling."

"That's what I'm doing big brother."

He looks at me with a disgusted expression. "I hate to hear that you are and I wish that you wouldn't. But if you are going to do it make sure you do it for yourself. Don't be out here hustling for no other hustler and be careful. I'm bout to head home and change clothes. Catch up with you later shorty!"

"Yeah no doubt, tell mom I will be home in a few."

I walk over to the pay phone and page Power. He calls me right back. "Yo I need to holla at you."

"I'm across the street, up in the building Rakim, come see me." As I step in the apartment, he is in the middle of doing a drug deal.

"Yo Rakim, sit tight for a second."

The Cubans have one guy at the door with a gun and another is walking around with a gun checking every room. The transaction is made; Power buys two kilos of cocaine.

"W'dup Rakim?"

"I need another ounce."

He pops a piece of rock off the brick and puts it on the scale until it reads 28 grams. I get my package and head home.

"There is my son, hey Rakim, your brother Marvin just went upstairs."

"Oh, yeah I saw him come in. Mom what you cook?"

"Some cornbread, butter beans, fried chicken and sweet peas."

"Ooh that sounds good; I'm a go upstairs to wash up for dinner."

* * * * *

The next morning as the sun comes up I wake up and meet Sham at the bus stop to roll up a blunt so we can catch the city bus downtown. We hit up a couple clothing stores buy a few pairs of kicks and head back to the block looking fresh. While sitting on the corner I have my headphones on listening to this new tape I bought by this rapper named Nas. This kid is hot! His lyrics are crispy and fresh. As the night falls, the police are busy tonight hitting drug houses. I turn it in early only for mom to be waiting on me with a look that means business.

"Rakim, where did you get them new clothes and shoes from in your closet?"

"Mom, I'm not gone lie, I bought them with money I earned hustling. I'm getting older mom, I can't wear them no name brand shoes and clothes to middle school."

"I'm going to tell you the same thing I told Marvin, you get your ass caught up out there selling drugs, don't call me cause I can't do nothing for you and do not bring that shit in my house. I taught you all better than that, I'm not gone let yawl worry me to death, Rakim."

I walk up stairs with shame and guilt on my face, I feel like I let my mom down. Even though I feel bad, I can't stop hustling like Marvin said this shit is addictive.

The next day my beeper goes off. When I call the number back it's one of my customers. He wants to spend $200, so I walk on the next block to meet him and collect my money. Afterwords I head to the corner of Garson Ave. Soon as I get there, I make a sale to someone I don't know. Five minutes later the police roll up on me. I throw thirty bags of coke under the steps of an abandoned house.

The police officer says. "Hey, you come here, put your hands up."

They frisk me the officer pulls 300 dollars out my pocket and goes under the steps where they find the drugs. While I'm in the back seat of the police car I can see my brother Marvin, my older sister Stephanie and the whole neighborhood watching as I am hauled off downtown to the county jail by the police. They lock me in a holding room for about an hour and I'm booked in on a sale charge at 13 years old. Guess who shows up to get me? My mom and step dad; they release me and give me a court date. As we walk in the house my mom gets straight down to business.

"Rakim what the hell did we just talk about yesterday? What is it going to be, the drugs or the music? You are headed down the wrong path. I can't keep my eyes on you and work too!"

I decided quickly. "The music mom."

"I bet not hear nothing else about you selling no drugs or me and you gone have a problem son."

As I walk upstairs I can just hear my mom cursing and raising hell about what happened. Three more weeks until school starts and the summer is winding down. I have a studio session today but my pager is steady buzzing. I walk up to Peck St. Park sit on the park bench and rolled up a blunt. I spark it up, sit back and just reflect on life and things that are happening around me. I look up and see Lil.B and O.G. Puk pass through in the fresh new Honda Accord, chrome wheels looking fly. It's getting dark out and the street lights are on. The police are busy tonight flying up and down the block with their lights on. I don't need to get bagged again by the police so I take a different route home. I cross East Main Street and see Marvin hanging out with his crew.

"Yo, w'dup big bro?"

"Wdup Rakim, where you coming from?"

"The park."

"Yo hurry up and get home, some stick up kids just robbed some kids up the street and shot both of them."

As I make it to my block I see the streets are lit up with lights. The police have ran up in the weed house three doors down and took everybody to jail in the house. My mom is standing on the porch, she looks at me and says "keep on, that's where your little ass going to be headed if you don't stop."

"Mom ain't nothing going to happen to me."

"Well, just keep it up son. You already have a court date pending."

I walk in the house and take a shower, I forgot to go to the studio today and I didn't even call Mike.

*****

It's a week later and my court date is today. I am being represented by a family friend. His name is Mr.Frazier.

"How are you doing today Rakim? I have already spoken to the judge, just plead guilty and I will handle it from there."

As I approach the judge, he reads me my charges and I plead guilty. He sentence's me to three months' probation and to take a trip up to Attica State Prison for a 'Scared Straight Program' at the end of my sentence.

We finally make it home from court and my beeper won't stop going off. I run out to make the three hundred dollars from a client on my beeper and come straight back home. I walk upstairs and turn on this new record by another new hip hop artist named Biggie. He's from Brooklyn and he's blowing up right now.

Shamar surprises me as he walks in the room. "How was court kid?"

"Everything good, got three months' probation. Yo, I hope you got your money stacked up. Ms.Shirley has a bus trip going to the city this weekend to go shopping. We can get some hot gear before we go back to school."

"Yea I'm good, I got a couple racks."

"Yo, we gonna be pulling out Friday around midnight."

"Be careful out their Rakim, some stick up kids been out robbing."

"Yeah, Marvin was telling me about that the other night on my way home."

Friday morning finally rolls around. I walk up on East Maine Street to get my hair cut at the Barber Shop. I see my family Little Nelson and his cousin Wayland, from New Jersey.

"Yo what's good fam? I see yawl got the fresh new cuts, looking wavy holding the block down."

"What's good Rakim. We just chillin'."

"Cool," I replied giving each of them a fist pound. "I'm a catch up with you cats later."

After an hour in Appleberry's Barber Shop I step out with the fresh cut. I get back to the hood up on Goodman, and I spot a blue Buick with three people in it that keeps circling the block. I look around the corner and one tries to jump out on me with a hoody on his head. I pull out my gun and fire three shots at the car. The guy jumps back in the car and they speed off towards Peck Street Park. I put the gun back in my pocket and run back across to Garson Ave where I see X.

"W'dup Rakim?"

"Yo some stickup kids in a blue car just tried to rob me I had to pull the heat out."

"Damn little shorty, you out here busting ya gun already."

After all of that drama, Sham and I spark up a blunt before we get ready to head into the city. I got my head phones on listening to Wu-Tang. As we pull into the city, I see the Statue of Liberty and all these big buildings. I see the Twin Towers. We park in Manhattan for a couple hours and shop, then head to Jamaica, Queens to load up on clothes and shoes. While hanging out in Queens we find a jewelry store and get top and bottom gold bridge plates for our teeth made. It's crowded, people are out everywhere. You can hear police sirens all over the city. After a long day of shopping, we stop at a Jamaican Restaurant and get some Jerk chicken and Jamaican beef patties. On the way out we pass through Castle Hill Projects in the Bronx. The scene looks just like I imagined it would.

"Yo, Rakim I got so many bags of clothes son, I feel like I'm leaving shit behind."

"Yeah me too Sham."

As we make it back to Roc City it's dark out. The crackheads are lurking and the hustlers are working. Everything was the same as when we had left earlier.

"Yo Shamar I missed another studio session with Mike again, damn I'm fucking up with this music."

"You done got addicted to this money, kid."

I head straight upstairs when I make it home. I am so tired, my bed is calling me. My beeper has been going off all day and night. I fall on the mattress and fall asleep instantly.

When I wake up it's seven o'clock the next morning and I can hear mama downstairs getting ready for work. I got money on my beeper that's steady calling. I see Marvin finally slept at home for a change. I put on my fresh white Adidas with a pair of Boss Jeans, a Nautica shirt and my gold rope, and then hit the block.

I knock on Shamar's room window. "Yo, come out son."

"I got one rolled up to smoke. What's good Rakim?"

"Cooling, trying to get all the money I can today. "I got some good weed to nigga."

"I got it from Power spot on Goodman. Shorty over there running the spot."

While up on the corner, Lil.B and O.G. Puk pull up.

"Yo wdup Rakim?"

"Just trying to get this money rude boy. I see you two riding good and smoking good."

"Wdup O.G.Puk?"

"Just cooling baby."

"Yawl be eazy, catch up with you later. The money is coming today the crackheads are everywhere."

"Yo Shamar, let's get a dice game going on. Me, Little Jay, Markus and Shamar got the dice game popping. All of a sudden we hear something that sounds like firecrackers continuously popping.

"Yo yawl heard that. Kid them sound like gun shots."

I step out to Webster Ave and look down the block. "Yo, somebody just got shot, let's walk down the block and see what's going on." As we get closer, the police have the street blocked off. "Yo I can't believe what I see, somebody done shot Lil.B and Puk while they were riding."

The car is riddled up with bullets with blood all over the seats. I think to myself as I sit there and watch both of my two close friends bleeding everywhere and gasping for air helplessly. The neighborhood is very upset, I never seen so much crying in one day; this is a very sad day for our community. As I walk inside my house I can hear the news. 'Two teens ambushed and shot to death on the east side of town today.' It's two weeks later and two of my closest friends have been buried and put to rest.

"Mom I'm leaving, I'm headed to the studio."

"Okay talk to you later Rakim."

I knew at a time like this I could make some good music. All of the pain I felt inside would take my mind off the street drama. Lil.B and Puk's murders reminded me that nobody ever knew what day God would call them. I planned to make something real tight in the studio today.

2011/12/12 15:32

CHAPTER EIGHT-DRUGS OR SCHOOL

Two years has passed. I only have three more days until High School. I jump off the city bus on Webster Ave and I see Power pull up in the Cherry red Lexus.

"W'dup Rakim?"

"W'dup witchu Power?"

"Just cooling."

"Let me hit that blunt."

"Yo Rakim, come here let me talk to you for a minute." He looked at me with his face drawn tightly." You gotta be careful it's a war going on. Brother's getting shot and murdered over these drugs. Since I first seen you back on Central Pk, I liked your style. Little Rakim you keep to yourself and you about your paper. Make sure you keep your head in them books and you gonna go far my nigga. These streets are only temporary remember that."

"No doubt Power, I appreciate that quick politic. I'm a get up with you. One love big bro."

I step cross Webster Ave and get to Garson, its police everywhere and they got the street blocked off. The police walk up to me and show me a picture of my home boy Markus and ask me have I seen him. The officer says he is a suspect in a murder case.

"No officer I haven't seen him."

I walk to the next block to get to my house. I walk inside and my sister Michelle has Markus hidden upstairs in our house.

"Yo what the hell you doing here? The police outside looking all over for you about a murder.

You gotta leave before my mama get off work."

"Yo Rakim, I can't leave right now its police everywhere."

You can hear the police knocking at our front door.

"They outside everybody be quiet."

They knock for about ten more minutes then go to the next house. About two hours pass before I address Markus again.

"Hey Mark, I'm bout to beep Power and when he calls back I'm gonna tell him to come get you."

About 45 minutes later, Power pulls up in the driveway and Mark jumps in the back seat and they pull off.

"Michelle, don't be letting nobody in this house when nobody home," I warned my sister.

"He was banging on the door Rakim, I didn't know what to do."

"When momma whoop yo ass, you gonna know what to do then I bet. You bet not open that door no more," I scolded my sister.

It's getting late, mama and I are sitting on the couch watching t.v. The news comes on. A picture of one of my neighborhood friends pops up.

I look at mama. "That's Marcus Dixon he has been shot and killed over his coat that was rewarded to him for his grades in school." My other friend Quentin Riddle witnessed the murder.

"Rakim, that's exactly why I preach to you, to be careful out in these streets. Tonight Marcus was murdered for no reason minding his own business."

The next day I'm up early ready for my first day at East High School. I got a pocket full of money and fresh new clothes. I get to school and while I'm sitting in third period class, all I could think about was the money that I was missing out on the block while here at school. By sixth period, I was on my way back to the block. I was addicted to getting this money. I get stopped by the police outside of the school. They check me for drugs and guns. They find nothing and let me go.

As the weeks pass, I slowly stop going to school and they end up kicking me out and sending me to an alternative school downtown called Josh Lofton. Getting ready for my new school I put my book bag on and head to the corner to catch the city bus. Josh Lofton is the type of school where anything could happen. The bus pulls up in front of the school and I'm greeted by Ms. Shirley.

"Good morning Ms. Shirley."

"How are you today, Rakim?"

"I'm good, looks like we gonna get some rain today."

I go to my first period class; At Lofton they are two hours long. As soon as the bell rings and I walk out in the hallway two girls started fighting. One pulls out a razor and cuts the other girl across the face. Giving her a buck fifty, blood is pouring everywhere.

"Yo, w'dup Doody? You see these females out here acting like they don't give a fuck.

"Yeah, Rakim it's crazy out here. This kid off the block shot my brother Rod the other day, every since Lil.B and Puk got killed it's just crazy out here."

"I feel you my fam. Yo, tell big bro Rod E Money Bags I said wdup. I'm bout to head out and catch this bus. Be safe."

I stop in Foot Locker on the way home and snatch me a pair of fresh Timberland, boots since the snow is starting to come down. They are setting up for Christmas already, putting lights all over the city and my beeper is steady buzzing. More money, more money, more money! I get to the block and make a quick $300.00 sale to one of my upscale customers.

I see my Code D. "W'dup Shamar? Where the fuck you been?"

"Yo Rakim, they had me locked up for three weeks for not going to see my Probation Officer. I just got home today."

"Yo Sham, we need to call dread and get some coke. I got us a house set up to hustle out of back behind the Arab store on Goodman. We can go in half on two ounces, that's twenty four hundred.

I'm a call Dread get the coke and meet you back up at the spot so we can bag it up."

I make it back to the block and its snow everywhere. "Yo, Shamar open the door its cold out here."

We break the coke down and bag it all up, next thing you know the crackheads are coming like clockwork. The next day I look out the window and its snow white. You can't see anything except snow. I put on some new shit by Jigga while I get dressed. He's running the air waves now. When I'm done getting dressed I go downstairs.

"Wdup mom? I see you setting up the Christmas tree, playing your blues."

"Yes I am; before you leave here I want you to shovel that snow out the drive way."

I cover up like an Eskimo and knock the driveway out, then head to the spot.

"Yo how much coke we got left Sham?"

"We almost out son."

"Yo, Power next door in the building over the store. Let's count the cash up so we can get some work from him before he leaves."

I take care of that situation, then stop up on the corner and make a quick 200 dollar sale off my pager. "Yo w'dup, X?"

"Just cooling Rakim. You know Bugs got shot up on Parsells Ave last night?

"I heard that."

He got caught up in the middle of a stick up and the police caught up with Mark, they tryin' give him 10 years for attempted murder."

"It's getting crazy out here, X."

"That's why I keep my gun on me; they got us under pressure out here."

"Yo I'm headed home X, catch up with you later tell Little Jay I said w'dup this snow starting to come down heavy kid."

As I walk down the Ave everybody is putting up their Xmas lights, brightening the block up for the holidays. I get home and walk inside.

"Hey mama, I see you got through with the Xmas tree, now all we need is some gifts."

"You got that right Rakim, we'll see if Santa comes to the ghetto this year."

I go upstairs and my brother is home. "Yo' Marvin wdup!"

"Not shit, me, Boe Cat, and B. Blast bout to go to the Jamaican Club and light up the bong bong, BiggaFord WebbZite performing at Water Street tonight."

"Okay check you later big brother."

The next day I get up and mom has decorated all the windows and there is even Xmas presents starting to build up under the Xmas tree. I get dressed like I'm going to school and head to the spot.

"Yo w'dup Rakim? Yo some niggas tried to kick the door in last night and rob the spot. I didn't have my gun on me so I had to jump out the upstairs window. I still got the money and the coke stashed upstairs."

"Yo Sham, keep your gun on you from now on. Niggas think they can just run up in here and take our shit, we gone put that heat on they ass next time they come knocking!"

"Yo light that weed up Rakim."

"After we finish with this last bundle of coke let's go shopping for some jewels, it's Xmas time nigga."

After a couple hours of hustling we hit the downtown mall up, snatch some new jewels and fresh gear.

"Yo Rakim, Xmas gone be here in two more weeks and it's already like a blizzard out here."

"Yo son my mom's been talking about moving down south."

"Why she wanna do that Rah?"

"She says it's too much craziness and madness going on out here."

"Damn Rakim, that's fucked up. You the only real brother that I got, me and you like bread and butter the hood Capone & Noreaga."

"Yea its crazy."

Two weeks later Xmas Eve is finally here and I haven't been to school in over a month. I can smell all the pies and cakes that my mom is baking downstairs for tomorrow; damn that shit smells good. My pager starts going off so I put on my coat on and walk downstairs.

"Mom I'm bout to go to the store, be back in a minute."

Everybody is outside playing in the snow, building snowmen and throwing snow ball's. I get to the corner and see the police, they have ran up in my boy X spot. I can see they have kick the door in with the k-9 in searching for drugs. They bring him out in handcuffs and put him in the back of the police car to take him downtown.

"Wdup Shamar, you see the police just hit X spot?"

"Yeah I see that shit, police been all over the hood today. Yo Rakim let's get some smoke and lay low for the rest of the day. On some real shit I can't believe you're going to be moving away after the winter is over."

"Yeah Shamar, we bout to get up outta New York. You ready for Xmas?"

"Yeah it looks like it's going to be a white Xmas with all this snow steady falling. Yo Rakim do you realize that me and you been through more shit in these streets than the average adult and we only 16 years old. Hard to believe we been doing this since 12 and 13 but it's true."

"Through all the shoot outs, our friends being murdered, drug deals niggas going to jail. My brother getting shot, your brother getting shot and we still out here that's a blessing kid. Yo, Rakim I got a kid on the way too, I just found out my girl pregnant."

"Wow Shamar, just make sure you do the right thing and hold it down. I'm bout to walk home I'm a catch up with you in the morning."

I walk in the house; it's lit up with lights and music. Everybody is still awake waiting on Xmas day to arrive. I get to the room and see Marvin is still up. "W'dup bro, I see you over there counting up all that dope boy money."

"I be seeing you and those Jamaicans over there getting that money on East Main Street.

"Rakim go to sleep and stop talking all that noise."

"Fine, good night grouchy Marv."

I wake up to kids running down stairs to open presents for Xmas and the smell of breakfast. It smells good too. I walk down stairs and greet everyone, "Merry Christmas mom and everybody!"

I can feel it; this is going to be one of them good days for the Jones family. My mother is on the phone with my grandmother from down south in Mississippi, everybody is just doing their own thing opening presents while the music is playing. There is a knock at the door and it's the Frazier boys. What's Christmas without Frazier Flav.

"Yo Marvin upstairs yawl go wake his ass up. Come on in Shamar, I see you looking fresh with the jewels shining. Happy holidays!"

"Yo Rakim you ready to roll one up?"

"Yeah let me get dressed."

We walk outside; the kids are all over the block having snow ball wars and trying to ride bikes in the snow.

"Let's walk up to the corner and smoke this blunt."

I see little Jay up on the block. "Damn Jay, you hustle on Christmas too."

"Yeah , I gotta get it. Let me hit that weed yawl smoking on. Yo, Rakim I was watching the news last night, these stick up kids tried to rob this nigga on Conkey Ave yesterday it's getting crazy in the city."

There go Power pulling up. He jumps out the white Pathfinder looking fly, jewelry blinging as usual.

"Merry Christmas everybody, I see everybody dress fly. Santa must have been good to the block."

Everybody starts laughing. "Yo I'm bout to walk to the store and go back to the house."

"Alright peace Rakim, catch up with yawl later. Merry Christmas my niggas, be safe."

I walk back inside where it's warm at, it's freezing outside. There is Christmas paper everywhere from all of the opened presents. Later on that night we have lots of family over and friends to play cards and drink with while listening to the blues and Christmas music.

The next morning snow is steady coming down. Marvin pulls out a brick of coke from the closet and breaks a chunk off of it.

"Where you headed Marv?"

"I got to go take care of something, check you later Rakim."

After Marvin leaves I go in the closet and break me a chunk off the brick too. I walk down to the drug spot, where Shamaris at.

"Yo w'dup Rakim?"

"Not shit, I just hit Marvin closet up. I'm bout to bag this half ounce of coke up right quick."

"Yo Rakim I'm bout to catch a cab to the Goodman Plaza to get some wings and Chinese food hold the spot down till I get back."

The money steady coming back to back, the crack heads act like they can't get enough of this coke. Then one of my normal customers from down the block knocks at the door.

"What's up Rakim?"

"Not much, what's up Hector?"

"Let me get a 100 dollars worth of coke Rakim, you mind if I take a little bump before I leave?"

"Nah go ahead."

I sit and watch Hector as he cooks up the coke on a spoon into crack and puts it on the tip of his crack pipe, lights it up and smokes it. All of a sudden he blows the smoke out his eyes get big. He just freaks out and starts hallucinating. He runs towards the window and jumps straight out, through the glass and everything. Then he just starts running down the street screaming. Shamar pulls back up in the cab.

"Yo, Rakim what happened to the window?"

"Yo Hector just came through and bought some coke. He smoked some in the house before he left, then he just flipped out and jumped out the window."

"Yo Rakim that must be that blue magic shit, got the dope fiends jumping out windows. Cocaine is a powerful drug to make his ass flip out like that what the fuck we gone do bout the window?"

"Get it fixed what you think."

CHAPTER NINE-LAST
DAYS ON THE BLOCK

As the spring starts to creep in, the snow is slowly starting to fade away and melt. My mom has been preparing and packing to move back down south. I walk up on the block and I see my whole crew out.

"W'dup Rakim?"

"W'dup X?"

"I heard you moving back down south."

"Yeah we gone be moving soon."

"Yo, Shamar w'dup kid?"

"Cooling, just got back from shopping."

"I see you shining with the new jewels and kicks looking crispy my brother."

"What you bout to do Rakim?"

"I'm headed up to the barbershop to get a haircut then I'm coming back to the block to try and get some of this money."

"Catch up with you when you get back."

I walk up to the barbershop, "yo wdup Doody?"

"Everything good fam, just got through getting a fresh cut. Yo Rakim, niggas been talking about yawl over there on Garson Ave, yawl boys getting that money."

"We just maintaining that's all, wdup with you."

"You know me, I'm headed to East Side Center to ball, so I can do somebody ass in on the court."

"You a wild boy, yo I'm a get with you Doody. Tell the family I said wdup."

"Alright, peace son."

I walk inside the barbershop, the new D.J. Clue mix tape is playing on the radio.

"What's going on Rakim? What kinda cut you want today?"

"You can give me that fresh Caesar."

"There you go shorty, got you looking fresh."

I reach in my pocket and pull out a big stack of cash and give the barber 30 dollars.

"Thanks for the tip. Damn shorty you got so much money you can't even fit it in your pockets."

I head back to Garson Ave and see all the drug dealers pulling their cars out today. Flexing real hard up on the corner, I see Shamar, Little. Jay and Shawny B. They got a dice game going on. Power pulls up flexing real big in the fresh painted money green Mazda 626, with the new chrome wheels.

"Yo w'dup Power?"

"What's going on Rakim?"

"You talk to Mark?"

"Yeah he's good; the Judge gave him a 10 year stretch. He'll be home soon."

"Tell him I said w'dup. Yo Shamar, light that purple haze up. I need to smell some green in the air today."

My beeper is vibrating and its money coming all day up on the block. Everybody is getting money today, the neighborhood is busy, and the Puerto Ricans are blasting their music.

"Yo Rakim, here hit the blunt."

Jamaican Dangles pulls up laying low key in the rental car; him and Marvin hop out. Dangles is smoking a big spliff talking in a deep Jamaican accent. "Whah gwhan my yute, every ting crisp hah rude boys."

While they all in the dice game, I'm steady serving the dope fiends getting this money. I see Dinnique, her cousin Precious and their little walking crew coming up the block.

"W'dup Dinnique, you ready to be my lady?"

"No Rakim, the question is are you ready to be my man?"

"I'm a get back to you on that; you put me on the spot."

"Yeah I bet I did, see you later Rakim."

I walk in the Arab store on the corner. "Yo, let me get a steak sub with boss sauce cheese and 2 Philly blunts to go."

I step out the store and look across the street; the police got my whole crew laid out on the ground again. The cops search them finding no drugs and make them throw away the dice. I walk across the street.

"Yo Sham, the police was trying to bag yawl up."

"Yeah man, I was scared as hell Rakim. I had my gun in my boot; they didn't even find it on me though."

"You lucky kid. Let's go sit on your porch so I can eat this sandwich."

"Yo Rakim, what up with the rapping and you going to the studio?"

"Man between out here hustling and a spotty attendance at school, I haven't had time to go. I know Mike think I let him down by not coming to the studio. Getting this fast money is addictive Shamar, it makes you don't want to do nothing but get money."

"Yo Rakim you nice with the rapping too, you need to start back going to the studio."

"Yeah I need to."

"Wdup Rakim?"

"Wdup Bridget?"

"About to braid Shamar hair and smoke yawl weed up. So roll up cause I know yawl got it."

While sitting on the porch we hear about three or four gunshots come from the next block over on Hayward Street. We walk over to the next block and there is a kid laid out on the sidewalk bleeding dead. He's been shot multiple times, the word quickly starts spreading through the neighborhood that Power shot and murdered him. Everyone from the hood is outside surrounding the dead body till the police and ambulance pull up and starts questioning people.

"Can you believe this Shamar, we all was just on the corner chilling together a few minutes ago rolling dice. Now the word is Power done murdered this kid, shit is crazy." Later on that night I'm sitting at home watching the news and Power picture pops up. They caught him in Buffalo, New York, at a Hospital; he was shot in the shoulder by the kid that he supposedly murdered.

The next day, the neighborhood doesn't feel the same. The police are all over the block, everybody is confused about what happened yesterday. A couple of weeks roll by and Power is released on bond with a murder charge pending.

While sitting at Peck Street Park one day, Power drives up in his all white pathfinder, gets out and fires up a blunt. "What's good Rakim?"

"Cooling, what's going on Power?"

"Just maintaining, so I guess you heard they trying' give me 25 years to life for that murder."

"Yeah."

"I heard you gone be moving back down to the dirty south."

"Yea, we gone be getting outta here soon."

"Yo, Rakim I just wanna drop a little jewel on you before you leave. I been watching you since you was a little shorty, back when your brother Marvin used to cut hair real heavy back in the day. You was always was a swift kid, always stayed solo, to yourself even hustling out here on these streets. You sharp with it, I like the way you and Shamar stick together and hold each other down. I slowly watched you step out into these streets and start to hustle. You a sharp little kid be careful out here, it's all kinds of jealousy and envy out in these streets. I see you going a lot farther in life than a lot of other brothers that's out here. You one of the good ones, cut from a different cloth than these other cats. I like your style little nigga, always remember fuck checkers play chess with these streets out here."

"Yo, Power, you one of the illest hustlers I ever seen do it in the drug game. I done watched you and your crew get a lot of paper out here on these streets. I learned a lot from yawl crazy niggas too."

"Yo, but I'm bout to get on the move, I got some money to collect. Rakim I'm a get up with you later I'm ghost, one love my nigga."

I sit back on the park bench and finish smoking the blunt then my beeper goes off, I got a customer that wanna spend three hundred dollars. So I walk back to the block to meet him and handle my business on the corner. I see Shamar hanging up on the corner.

"W'dup Rakim?"

"Cooling, I'm bout to head home and put some of this money up. I got about $1500 on me."

"Damn, Rakim you a hustling ass little dude. You ready to go tear the mall up now kid?"

"Yeah it's about time to go shopping, spend some dough, and get some new clothes. Shamar I'm a catch up with you, I'm headed home."

"W'dup mama?"

"Nothing still trying to get all this stuff packed and labeled."

"So what's the word on where we gone be living down south?"

"Your step father has an offer for a job at the rail road in New Orleans. So it's either going to be there or Mississippi, we still working on it."

"Okay well I'm headed up stairs."

I count my money up and stash it in my uncle old church suits that are hanging in the closet. I hear this beat coming from the TV and sit down and watch this video that's on B.E.T. by a rap group called The Ghetto Boys. It's called 'My Minds Playing Tricks on Me,' there from Houston, Texas.

"Yo, w'dup Marvin, you moving down south with us?"

"Nah I'm staying."

"I wish I could stay too."

"Rakim you can go down there and ride you some horses and catch you some chickens and live the farm life."

"Ya trying to be funny? I asked as I hear somebody downstairs knocking on the door.

"Yo w'dup Sham?"

"Not shit, me and Little Jay just shot at some stick up kids through the cut. We had to run they ass off the block trying to hustle. W'dup Marvin?"

"Nothing much just cooling. Shamar you out there letting your gun go off, huh?"

"You know me Marv, if the gun on my waist I got me a case."

"I hear that shorty."

The next day while up on the block rolling dice, Shamar pulls up in a new truck.

"Yo get in."

"You and them stolen cars."

"Naw it's not stolen, rented it from a dope fiend Jump in Rakim."

"I like this, how many days you got it?"

"I got it for three days."

"Let's go get us an ounce of weed off Hudson Ave."

"We bout to ride all over the city in this motherfucker, Rakim."

Shamar comes out with the weed. "Yo break that weed up Rakim. Roll us up a fat one."

"No doubt kid."

We cruise through the west side of town smoking, eyes blood shot red.

We decide to stop at the mall.

"Let's go in here and get some fresh new kicks. I got a couple hundred on me."

We go in NYC Clothing. I grab 3 boxes of kicks, 5 pairs of jeans and a couple sweaters. I was going to grab some jewelry but decided against it. I figured I could save the money.

"Yo Shamar, I like that leather bubble Phat Farm jacket son, this shit is hot."

"Right Rakim."

We head out the mall and jump back in the truck. It probably was a bad idea to smoke while we were driving but we did it anyways. We were the young and reckless.

"Yo Shamar I need to catch up with Power and get me some coke when we get back on the block."

"Light that weed up."

We pull up on Garson Ave and the whole crew is out. "Who the hell gave you two little rugrats keys to drive."

"Yo X, you seen Power?"

"Yeah he across the street in the building."

"Yo Shamar, I'll be right back. I'm going across the street to handle my business."

I get up stairs he opens the door. "W'dup Power, I need two ounces of coke."

"Just give me 2 grand even Rakim, you good on the rest."

"Appreciate that Power."

"Remember what I said Rakim, chess not checkers baby."

"No doubt."

I jump back in the truck "yo Sham drop me off at the house . I'm bout to go bag this work up and I got a couple customers to go serve. I'm a catch up with you later my nigga."

"Alright peace."

I go upstairs and put all my bags up. I bag up my coke fast because my mom will be in soon from work. Back out to hug the block and get this money. I got my headphones on listening to this new mixtape from the Lox, while I'm out hustling. Today the money has been constantly flowing like U.P.S. the sun is starting to go down. I hear sirens going through the city. At night time is usually when the city comes alive and all the madness starts. So everybody keeps their guns on their waist out on the block in case stick up kids wanna come through and try to stick us up.

Shamar pulls up in the truck, "yo w'dup son?"

"Not shit, out here getting this money."

All of a sudden about a dozen gun shots rang out. "Damn Rakim, you heard that? Somebody getting loose with the cannon tonight, the police will be flying through here in a few minutes."

"Yo Rakim, you seen my little brother Mike today?"

"Yea I seen his little ass earlier, he was up here hanging out on the corner."

"Oh okay, I bought that little nigga some kicks from the mall today."

"Yo I'm bout to get up off this corner before the cops come lurking, catch up with you in the morning."

I walk in the house my mom, all my brothers and sisters are on the couch watching The Cosby Show.

"What's up Rakim?"

"Nothing hey mom, why are we moving down south?"

"Rakim it's just too much killing going on in the city, the young black youth are just killing each other or going to prison. I don't know what I would do if I was to lose one of my kids to these streets. My mother, who is your grandmother, is getting older Rakim. I would like to spend her last couple of years with her. I just want a better place for my kids to grow up in and have a future; New York has just gotten too bad out here for young black men."

"I hear that ma. Well I'm bout to go upstairs in the attic and spin some records."

"Rakim keep the music down."

"I hear ya."

I got this new Mobb record and this new Foxy record. I put my earphones on and turn my music up. After an hour of mixing music, I see this new hood flick come on TV called 'Juice' starring 2Pac. I close the downstairs door, lift up the window and fire the blunt up. As I sit and look out my window the block is lit up, the Puerto Ricans are across the street partying. The white and black neighbors are out smoking weed on the sidewalk, I'm going to miss this place. From the age of 13 to 16 years old, I swear I have been through and seen more shit than a 35 year old out here on this block but I guess life goes on. As I puff the weed and blow the smoke out the window, I see Shamar come flying through in the truck blowing the horn. The next morning I put on my fresh white kicks with some Sean John jeans, and head towards the bus stop to catch the city bus to school downtown. The bus pulls up and the morning routine is the same.

"Morning Rakim."

"Morning Ms. Shirley."

The bus lets me out downtown in front of the school.

"Yo w'dup, Doody?"

"Damn Rakim, you finally brought your ass to school kid."

"Yea man, trying to learn a little bit today. I'm about to head to class, catch up with you later my homie."

I actually stayed in class all day today, which was surprising. Shamar scoops me up after school. He looks tired like he's been up all night.

"Wdup Rakim?"

"Not shit, what the money looking like on the block?"

"Shit been slow all day, police been riding the block."

"Blaze up Shamar. I hear you playing that new Noreaga joint."

"Yea that's my shit Rakim."

"Yo, drop me off in the hood."

I get out at the corner of the block and I see Big Shawn sitting out in front of his building.

"W'dup Rakim?"

"What's good Shawn?"

"Just cooling and maintaining. Be careful out here Rakim, the police been rolling today."

"Yeah I heard that, I'm bout to head to the house. Holla at you later fam."

I could always smell my mom's cooking before I even went in the house. I wanted to stop what I was doing and eat whatever she had to offer. I peeped in the kitchen.

"What you got to eat in them pots ma, whatever it is it smells good?"

All the pictures are off the wall, we got boxes packed and stacked neatly. It just doesn't seem real that we're gonna be moving.

CHAPTER TEN- 13 GOING ON 35

A couple months roll by and it's June. School is out and my mom finally got everything packed for the big move. The U-Haul truck is backed in the driveway. I walk up to the corner to finish selling the rest of the drugs that I have left.

"Yo w'dup Little Jay?"

"Just cooling, so you bout to head south?"

"Yeah we gone be leaving tonight."

"Yo Rakim, remember we both born October 18, 1978, two brothers from another mother. You my boy for life."

"No doubt Jay, I got you."

"Yo X, let me hit that weed."

I sit and hustle on the corner for a couple hours before the news comes through the block that they just gave Power 25 years to life for that murder. Shamar pulls up.

"Yo w'dup Rakim? I see you with the new linen on looking fresher than ever, with the white crispy kicks. "

"I'm just cooling."

"Out here getting this paper. Jump in Rakim let's go blaze a couple before you get outta here."

We back in Shamar's driveway and break down the Philly and roll up.

"Yo Rakim, you really bout to bounce from New York."

"Yeah bout to leave the fast life to you cats."

"Yo Rakim, you gone always be my boy for life. When I shine you shine, I wish you luck on your new journey my nigga."

"Thanks kid. Hey Sham remember when you used to spray paint Kid.1 all over the city and buildings."

"Yeah, I remember that shit."

We both start laughing, as I sit back and hit the weed.

"Yo I'm a miss this block, especially the summers here in New York and all the craziness that goes on here."

"Well Rakim I'm bout to bounce, if I don't see you before you leave fam, hold it down. I'll still be holding the Roc when you get back. Peace my nigga."

"No doubt son, one."

I chill out on the block all day, just about till night fall and finish off my last bag of coke. As I roll me up a blunt and spark it up, I see the police fly pass the block with their lights on. Word spreads up the block quick, somebody just got shot two blocks over. I put on my head phones and head towards my house, I see Marvin chilling in the drive way.

"Wdup big bro?"

"Just cooling, yawl bout to get ready to pull outta here."

"Yo Marvin, be careful out here."

"No doubt Rakim, you know me I move in silence like dead people."

"Yo you a smooth nigga, that's why these cats love yo style."

"I hear you little brother."

"Remember Marvin, don't play checkers with these niggas play chess. We cut from a different cloth that niggas don't understand."

"Rakim, we ready."

"Yo, one love big bro, we bout to be out."

"Alright Rakim, yawl be safe love you little bro."

As we pull off from 301 Garson Ave everybody is out running up and down the block. The streets are lit up and busy just like the first night we moved on the block. We get to the corner and I can see the whole crew out still hustling on the block. We hit the interstate and ride for miles and miles. Traveling through Pennsylvania, Ohio, Kentucky, and Alabama a day later, we find ourselves in the middle of southern Mississippi. Pulling up to my grandmother's house 806 North Magnolia St, we are greeted by lots of family members.

I see my grandmother, who I haven't seen in years and give her a big hug and kiss. Everybody's accent is very country and southern. My grandmother has prepared a big meal, all kinds of sweets; cakes, pies, butter beans cornbread, fried chicken, cabbage, sweet yams, sweet peas, and some southern style macaroni and cheese. After getting my stomach full, I walk outside and talk to a few of my cousin's to find out that they don't have cabs or city bus transportation out here. Either you have a car or you walk and it feels like it's 110 degrees outside. I'm so hot I'm confused.

Later on that day I finally get to see my real father, who I would always talk with on the phone, but hardly ever got a chance to see. That evening I go down to my dad's office. When I walk in I can tell he is very happy to see me. He has this big smile that's genuine; I give him a firm hand shake. We have a very deep father and son conversation about life, treating people right and being a man of your word. He just gave me so much knowledge and encouragement that would last me a life time in one hour. He reminded me of Martin Luther King when he spoke. After a year in Mississippi my family packs up and moves to New Orleans. My stepfather lands a good

job working on the rail road. The city reminds me of New York. The way the kids talk and dress the swag is so New York. The hip hop scene is very different. Cocaine and heroin is very bad here, the kids as young as 14 are addicted and it's being called the murder capitol. Here I dabble in and out of the crack game for a couple years. On February 16 2000, I was blessed with a baby boy, my first son at the age of 22. His name is Jaleen C Wilkinson; a few months after he was born I move back upstate to Lockport New York an hour away from Rochester New York, where I grew up as a kid.

I jump back in the drug game with my cousin on my side and everything seems to be running smooth. One day while up in Rochester, New York, I walk in the corner store on the West side of town to get two Phillies and I bump into Shamar who I haven't seen in a couple years. His hustle game is not at its best, so I bring him up to Lockport New York and put him back on his feet. Now we both getting money and living good again like back in the days. A year passes by and everything has been running like a well-oiled machine.

One snowy night there is a bunch of noise rumbling in my building coming up the stairs. All of a sudden I hear a loud boom at the door. The narcotics unit has kicked my door in with the K - 9 and laid everybody down and searched the house looking for drugs. They find a big bag of coke stashed in the computers printer. They take me down and book me with possession of control substance.

The next morning two officer's come get me from my cell and drive me somewhere upstate in a snow blizzard to go to court and I'm brought back to Lockport, New York where I sat in jail for a while. Finally I'm released and I sit down and have a long talk with myself and God. I promised Him that I'm done selling coke. I look back on my friends that I lost to the streets. During my time in jail I thought about the things that I had been through in life and how lucky and blessed I am to still be here.

One year later I find myself packing up in a U-Haul, headed back to New Orleans to start over. The road trip was 24 hours; I finally pull into the Crescent City. I stay with moms for a month, and then get me a nice apartment on the west side of the city working at doing maintenance work at a hotel. Every other week I jump in my car and drive down to Mississippi to visit my grandmother and father, it's only an hour and a half drive from New Orleans. I've been living here in New Orleans about four or five years now, all my brothers and sisters are here too. I got an offer for a construction job in Mississippi making good money, so now I'm packing up and heading further south to Mississippi. As I'm packing up to move from New Orleans there is an announcement that a hurricane is moving in, called Hurricane Katrina and they are warning us it's going to be a very bad storm and it's headed right towards us. I get to Mississippi and get moved in. A week later, the storm is steady moving closer.

My mom and the rest of the family are packing to leave New Orleans heading to Mississippi. The storm finally hits, it floods the city of New Orleans and tears up parts of southern Mississippi and the Gulf Coast. We are without lights and water for five or six days and it's hot as hell outside. We are getting reports of dead bodies floating in the city. A week later, finally the lights and water come back on, we turn the TV on and people are still waiting for help in New Orleans and still walking through the water. We have been receiving calls from all our family and friends back in New York making sure we are okay. Into the second week, the Mayor announces that it's safe to come back to the city to check on your property and loved ones. We drive down to check on my moms and sisters homes. They are flooded with water; they have army tanks, helicopters and soldiers everywhere. It almost seems like we are in a third world country. We get everything that we can salvage and move my mom and sister back to Mississippi and get them moved into their new homes.

My real father and I have been getting very close; he has taught me about being a man, being responsible and working hard for what you want and being respectful. Three weeks after Hurricane Katrina, Marvin and I fly back to New York on vacation to visit for a week. Shamar and I link up as soon as I get in town. He's still living the life of a hustler. He pulls out two shoe boxes full of money and throws me a couple stacks; we hit the city and go shopping like back in the day blazing up and reminiscing about old times. We drive through the old block Garson Ave; it looks like a suburban neighborhood now. It's nice and quiet, no hustlers are on the block.

Shamar asks, "You remember when we use to hang out on this block heavy?"

"Yea, that was the good oh days."

While hanging out on the old block I see my brother's older daughter Marqueena. She runs over and gives me a hug. I see Little Jay hanging out up on Hudson Ave doing his thing, we smoke reminisce and politic for a minute. The city is really different now; the police patrol a lot more. The young kids are killing each other at a fast rate now. A lot of the old hustlers are dead or in jail, very few are still walking the streets. While in New York those couple of days, I got a chance to see a lot of old friends and family. I also was able to get some good fried chicken, Philly steak and cheese with boss sauce.

We fly back south and return to the southern life style, no drug dealing or hustling, just hard work and family bonding. My father passed away September 12, 2009, right before my daughter was born. Just in the short time we bonded, he taught me so much about being a man. Shortly after, I was blessed with a beautiful baby girl. We named her Maliyah, after the president's daughter. She's six years old now, her and my son keep me on the right path.

Fast forward Its 2015, I'm back living in NY. I have a little side business that I started with my cousin, I. I have started my own book publishing company. I no longer deal drugs; I hustle a different way now. The legal way; just last month I turned 35 and the world is steady changing. I just made it in from a flight back from Mississippi from seeing my mom and kids. I get letters from

Power every now and then; he's locked up in Attica State Prison, somewhere in upstate New York. Shamar and I still talk every other week. He's still here in NY doing his thing. My brother Marvin works in the oil fields, he lives in Mississippi. My whole family is doing well now. You can catch Little Jay still doing his thing up on Hudson Ave. I politic with, X at least once a month now. Shamar's little brother, Michael was murdered in 2008 in New York, he's somewhere in heaven smiling down on us. I still see Markus & Shawny.B from time to time. My close friend Doody (Shavar Jamal Lewis) past a way in a senseless murder down in Florida 2 months ago that left his family and friends in the city very upset.

I am currently working on my second book titled 'Tale Of A Huztler' and just enjoying life with my kids. I talk to a lot of young urban kids whenever I get a chance to. To give them the inspiration that you can do whatever you set your mind to do, all things are possible if I can do it, you can do it. Sometimes we all have to go through the negative to get to the positive, just remember all my young urban youth no matter what you go threw in life you can always turn negative into positive. No matter what your past is let my story be an open door to your positive new way of life and living positive over negative.

Written By Author God-Son...

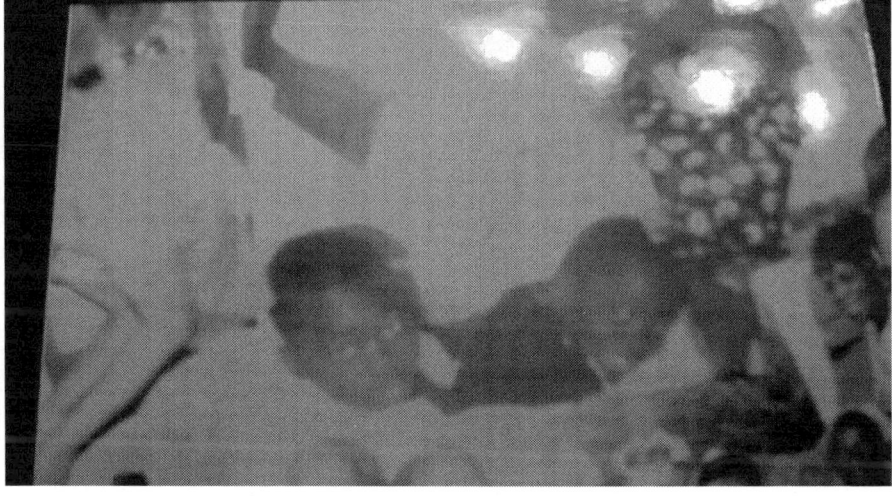

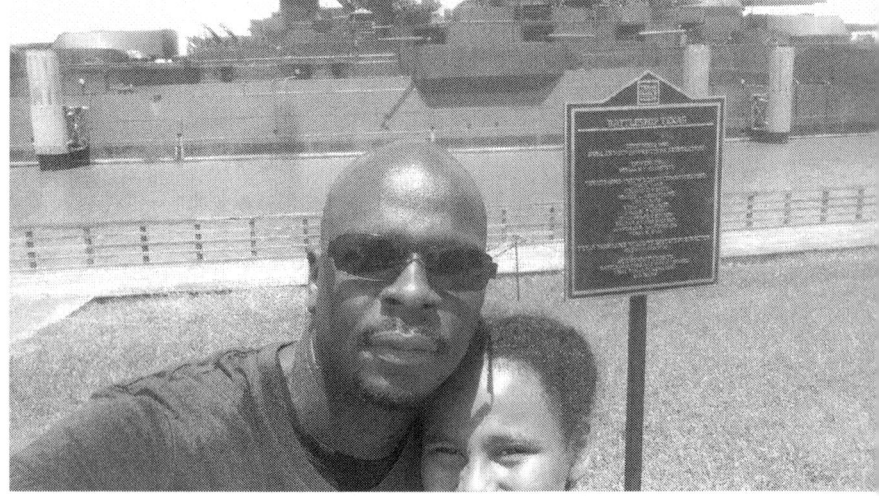

THE J.WILKINSON STORY

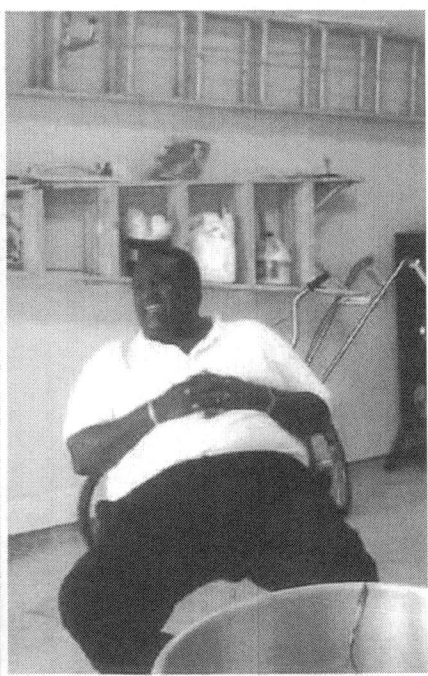

It's a challenge for Johnnie Melo
Sr. raising his only son who
carries his same name, in the
same streets from which he
overcome. But Johnnie Melo Jr.
will take his own path in life.
That path will determine his
existence on this earth. This is a
story of Love, Family, and the
Streets.

Writer & Director - Winston Young
Producer & Cinematographer - Carl Madison

WINNIE PRODUCTIONS INC.
WWW.WPIMOVIES.COM

KILLING THE FUTURE

DVD

JASON
VAHVEH

TYSHAY
TAYLOR

JOVAN
POWERS

KILLING
THE FUTURE

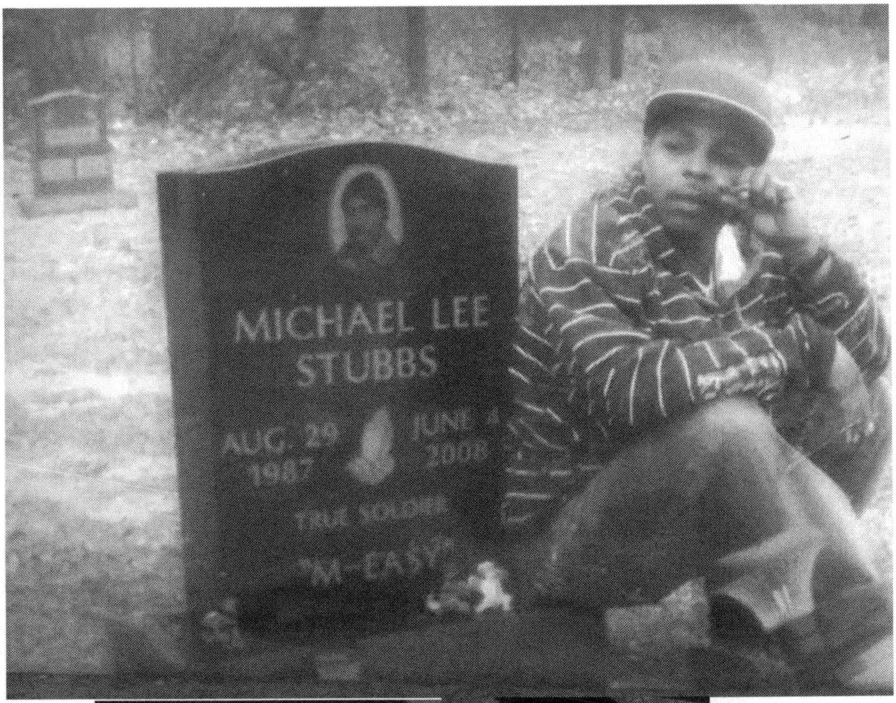
MICHAEL LEE
STUBBS
AUG 29
1987
JUNE 4
2008
TRUE SOLDIER
"M-EASY"

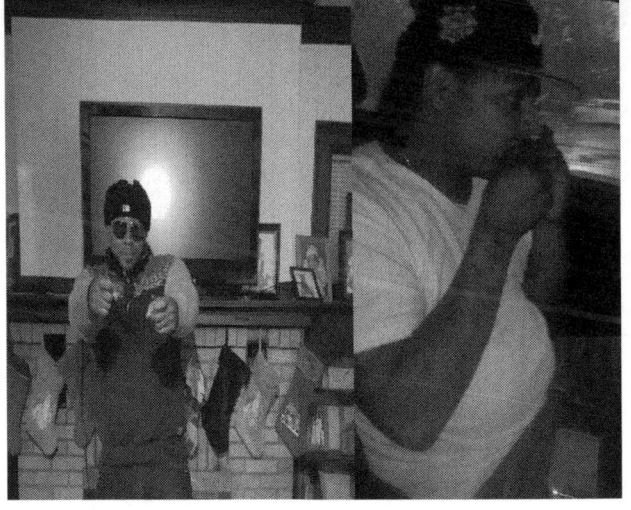

You'll Forever Be Missed! R.I.P.

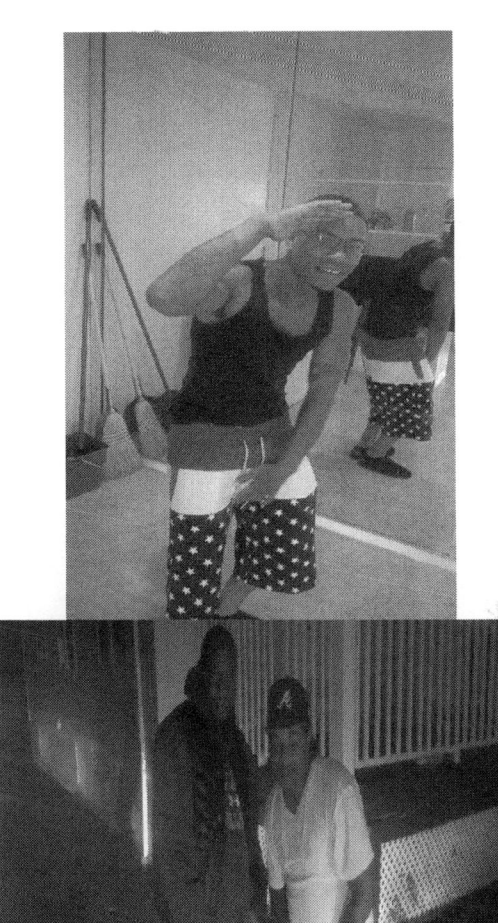

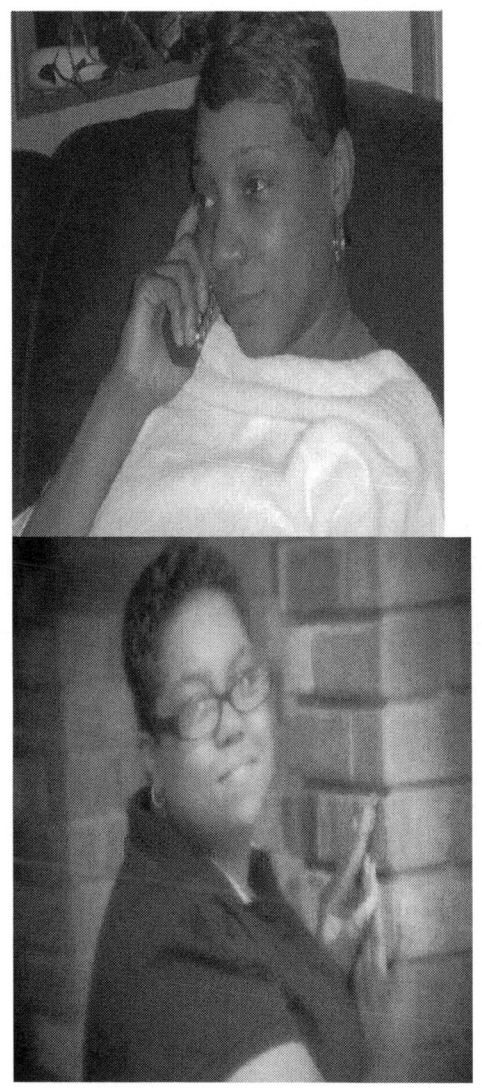

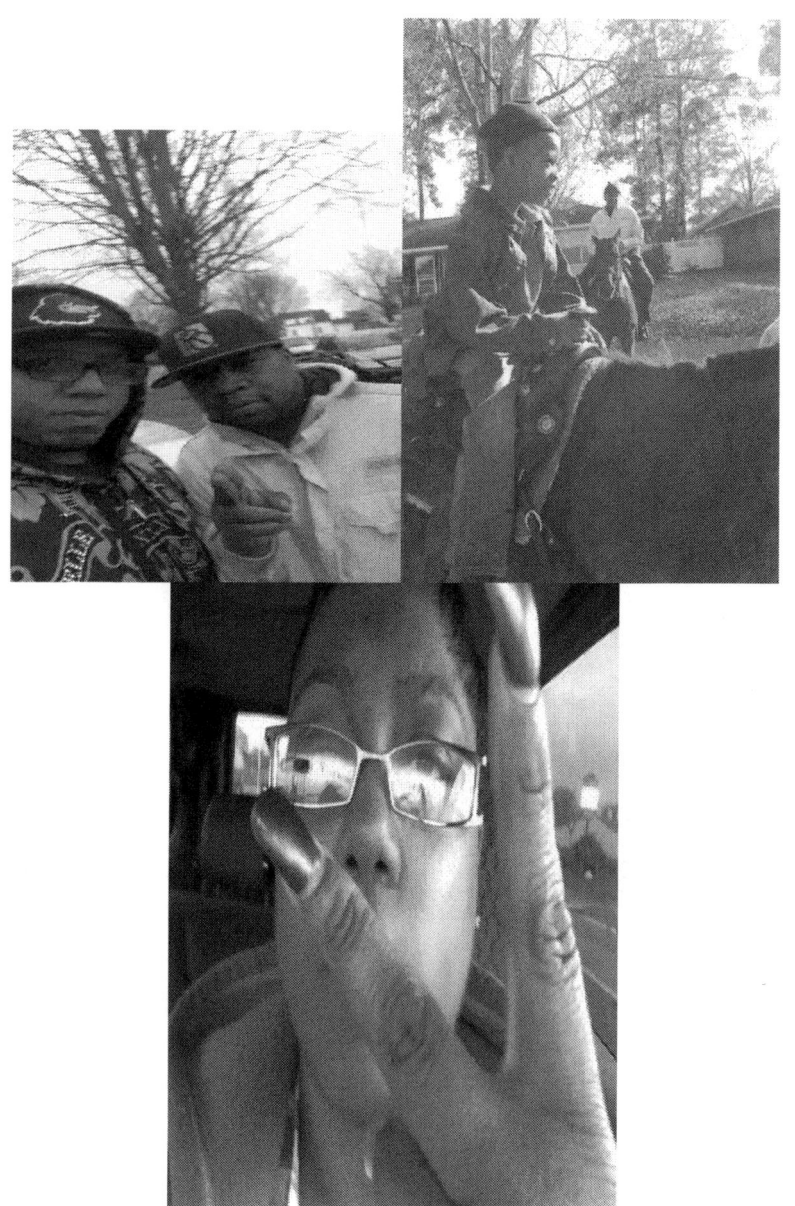

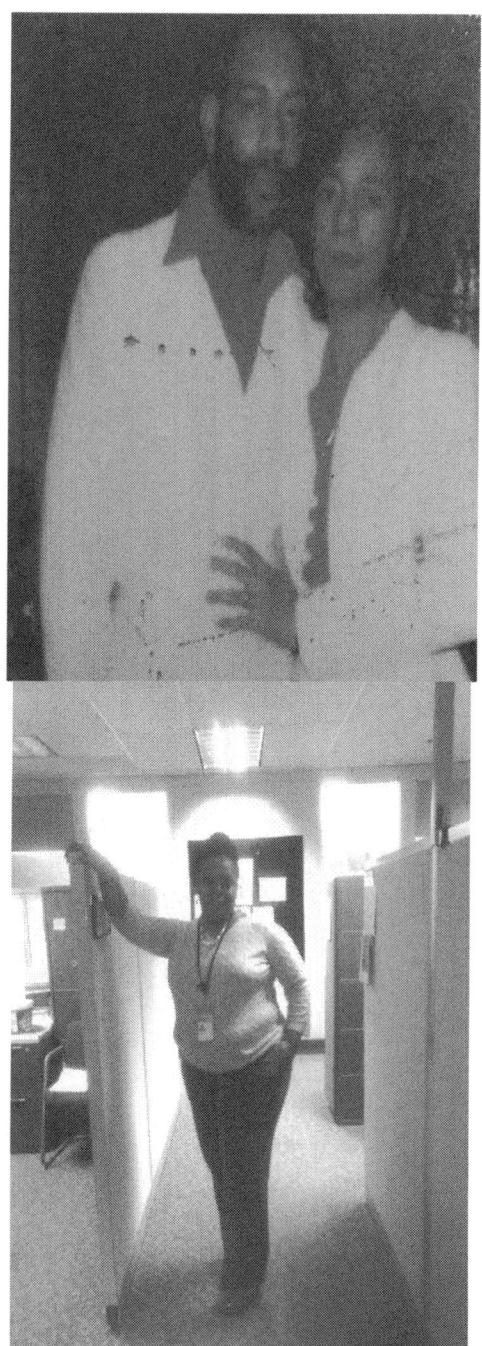

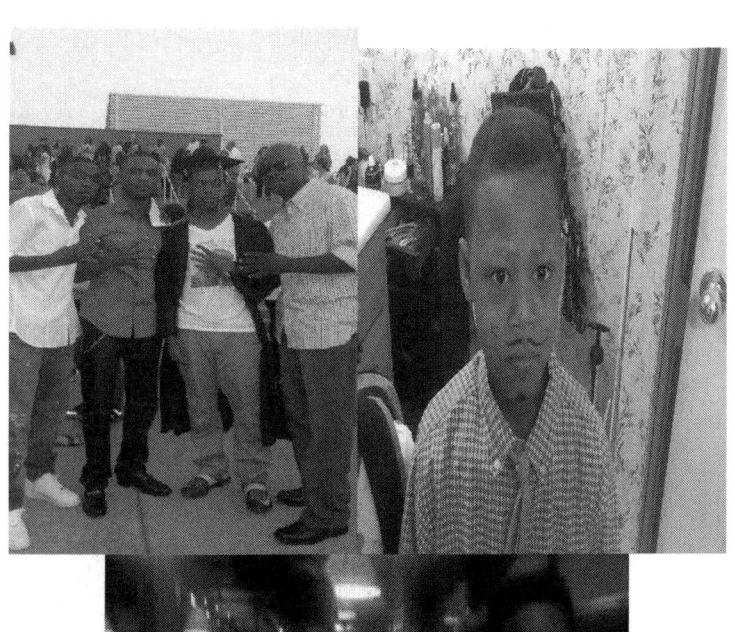

payperouteclothing

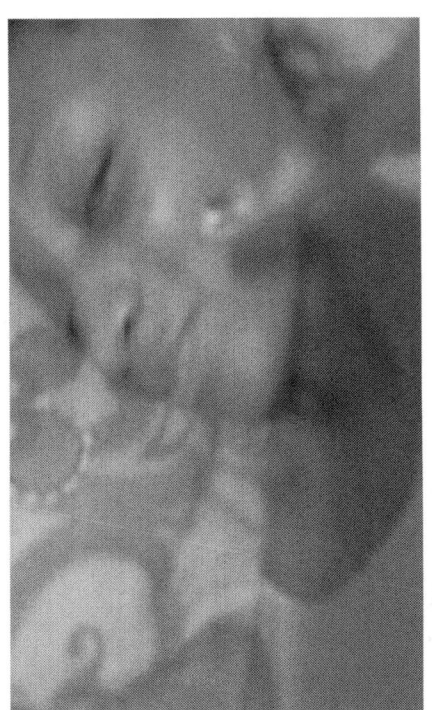

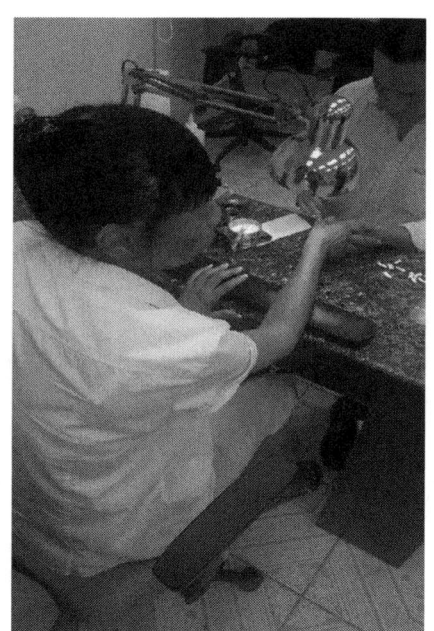

ACKNOWLEDGEMENTS

First of all I would like to thank the most high for just giving me life and chance at life in this cold world. Second I would like to thank my mother Barbra Ann Turner for setting a foundation for her seeds that still remains solid love you ma. Thank you to my grandmother Elaine P. Hampton who shared so much knowledge wisdom and understanding with all her encounters may you rest in peace. I would most definitely like to give a shout to my Pops John C. Thomas up in Heaven who gave me this hustle to grind and hustle no matter what obstacle you have in front of you love you Pops. Last but not least to everyone that support me while um at the bottom you know who you are shout to PRC nothing but motivation...

To TiT

From Author

GoD's Son

Thanks

For the support

Rocky City

Made in the USA
Middletown, DE
18 April 2016